COAST
WATCHING
IN WORLD WAR II

Other titles in the Stackpole Military History Series

COAST WATCHING
IN WORLD WAR II

Operations against the Japanese on the Solomon Islands, 1941–43

Edited by A. B. Feuer

Foreword by Walter Lord

STACKPOLE
BOOKS

Published in paperback in 2006 by
STACKPOLE BOOKS
5067 Ritter Road
Mechanicsburg, PA 17055
www.stackpolebooks.com

Printed in the United States of America

10 9 8 7 6 5 4 3 2 1

FIRST EDITION

Library of Congress Cataloging-in-Publication Data

Coast watching in World War II : operations against the Japanese on the
Solomon Islands, 1941–43 / edited by A. B. Feuer.— 1st ed.
    p. cm. — (Stackpole military history series)
Includes index.
Originally published: Westport, CT : Praeger, 1992.
ISBN-13: 978-0-8117-3329-8
ISBN-10: 0-8117-3329-7
1. World War, 1939–1945—Campaigns—Solomon Islands. 2. World War,
1939–1945—Communications. 3. Aircraft spotting—Solomon Islands—
History—20th century. 4. World War, 1939–1945—Personal narratives,
Australian. 5. Read, Jack, 1904– —Diaries. 6. Mason, Paul, 1900–1971—
Diaries. I. Feuer, A. B., 1925– II. Read, Jack, 1904– III. Mason, Paul,
1900–1971. IV. Series.

D767.98.C56 2006
940.54'26592—dc22
2006004624

This World War II narrative is dedicated to the Australian Coast Watching Service; to the land, sea, and air veterans of the battle of Guadalcanal; to the brave Solomon Islands missionaries; and—last but not least—to the loyal Bougainville natives, without whose help there might never have been an American victory at Guadalcanal.

Table of Contents

Photographs following page 108

Maps

Foreword

The first six months of the Pacific war were dark days for the Allied cause. Japan was sweeping south, almost unopposed. Hong Kong fell on Christmas Day, 1941 . . . Manila on January 3 . . . Rabaul on January 23 . . . Singapore on February 1.

By April 1942 the Japanese were lapping at the Solomons, the magnificent chain of islands that stretches from Bougainville, just below the equator, to San Cristobal, some 600 miles to the southeast. The next step would mean more than gobbling up territory. The Solomon Islands were like a fence guarding Australia only 800 miles away. If the Japanese gained a foothold in the Solomons, they could block the convoy routes between the United States and Australia.

Facing this terrifying onslaught there reeled a dispirited mob of Allied troops with their air and naval units and many demoralized civilians. The Japanese seemed unstoppable. Everyone wanted only to clear out. Or, that is, almost everybody.

As the rest fled, a tiny group of men faced the other way to confront the problem. They were very much a mixed bag: soldiers, naval personnel, traders, planters, missionaries, colonial officials, and "locals." Nearly all were thoroughly familiar with the area; many considered the South Pacific their only home. They had volunteered to stay behind and report on Japanese troop and ship movements, using portable teleradios that seem absurdly cumbersome by today's standards. These diehards were members of the Australian Coast Watching Service, headed by Lieutenant Commander Eric Feldt of the Royal Australian Navy. They were called "coast watchers."

There were about 100 coast watchers in the South Pacific altogether, with about 24 of them in the Solomons. Two of these men were stationed on Bougainville, the most exposed island in the chain, only 200 miles from the big new Japanese air and naval base at Rabaul.

For Jack Read, who covered the northern end of Bougainville, and for Paul Mason, who covered the southern end, life was always tense. Capture meant certain execution, but they were not allowed to take any offensive action themselves. Their mission was to observe, not fight. To drive home the point, the code word for the Solomon Islands coast watching activities was FERDINAND, named after the fictional bull who preferred flowers to the arena.

Jack Read was a dark, wiry, brisk man who had been in the New Guinea public service for 12 years. When war broke out, he was Assistant District Officer at Sohano, near the northern end of Bougainville. He took on the job of trying to evacuate the European community—mostly planters and missionaries—who had lived on the island for years and couldn't imagine going anywhere else.

Paul Mason was a small, owlish-looking man whose round spectacles gave the impression that he was a meek bank clerk. Actually he was anything but that. Strong as an ox, he had been manager of the Inus Plantation on the east coast of Bougainville for years and knew the islands inside out. He was an excellent radio technician, and, even more important, he knew and understood the native population.

Supporting these two coast watchers on the island was a small Australian commando unit that had originally been assigned to guard an Allied airstrip being built on Buka, a "satellite" island just north of Bougainville. The Japanese had quickly occupied the strip at the beginning of their advance, and now the commandos were hiding in the interior.

The only other friendly presence on Bougainville was a small group of natives who had remained loyal to the planters and the colonial government. These people became ever fewer as the Japanese strengthened their hold on the island. Read and Mason moved from hill to hill, somehow managing to keep up a steady flow of intelligence. But it wasn't easy. Besides the ever more aggressive Japanese, they faced the implacable jungle. Once away from the coast, the whole island was a mass of tangled vines, huge leaf plants, slippery mud, steep hills, mosquitoes, rain—and still more rain. There were no roads, not even paths, just faint trails known to a few of the natives.

There were no reliable maps, either. The first air drop of supplies fell 70 miles off target. Paul Mason had to borrow a bicycle from a missionary, then struggle 70 miles to the drop site, only to discover that there was nothing there. Then it was another 70 miles back again.

No wonder that one coast watching candidate, after hearing of the hardships and dangers, asked Lieutenant Commander Feldt, "Are there any special benefits that go with this duty?" "No," answered Feldt, "the only thing I can promise you is the promise of certain peril."

But this was enough for Jack Read and Paul Mason, whose reports from Bougainville have been so skillfully edited by Bud Feuer for this book. Mr. Feuer has wisely let them stand as written, and this, in turn, gives them an immediacy that no secondhand account could ever convey.

Walter Lord

Preface

This book is a compilation of edited accounts of the coast watching operation on Buka and Bougainville Islands in the South Pacific during the early part of World War II. It is primarily the remarkable story of Jack Read and Paul Mason and their struggle for survival in the Japanese-infested jungles of Bougainville. Jack Read and Paul Mason's accounts were edited from microfilm reports on file at the U.S. Naval Historical Center in Washington, D.C. Included in Read's report are reports by Jack Keenan, V. Day, and G. McPhee.

I would like to thank the many people who contributed their time and efforts to provide accounts of their adventures on Bougainville Island, particularly, Ken Thorpe, Douglas Otton, Jack Read, Walter "Lucky" Radimey, and Sister Mary Irene Alton. I also wish to thank Noelle Mason (Mrs. Paul Mason) for her Afterword concerning Paul Mason and his experiences on Bougainville.

I would also like to recognize coast watcher Martin Clemens, Reverend George M. Lepping, S.M., and the many members of the Guadalcanal Veterans Association who provided valuable information.

A special thanks to Walter Lord for writing the Foreword, and to Ted Blahnik, editor of *Guadalcanal Echoes*, for permission to use Walter Radimey's amazing article that appeared in the April 1989 issue of the *Echoes*.

The South Pacific: The Solomon Islands and Vicinity

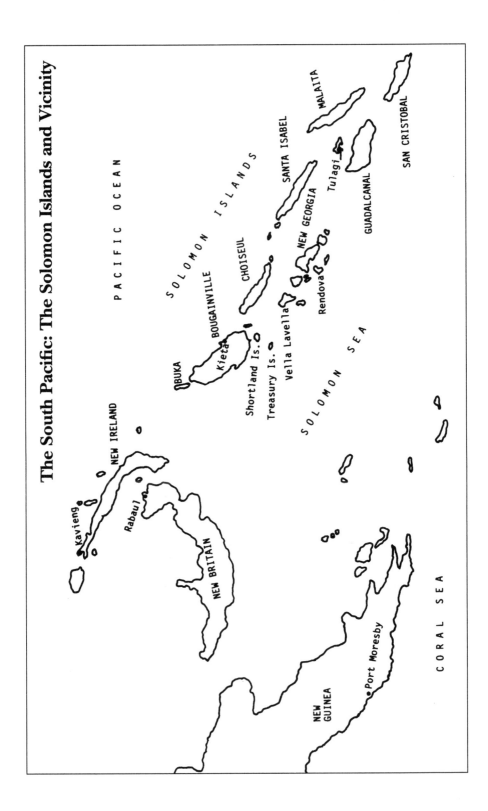

PACIFIC OCEAN

SOLOMON ISLANDS

NEW IRELAND

Kavieng

Rabaul

NEW BRITAIN

BUKA

Kieta

BOUGAINVILLE

Shortland Is.

Treasury Is.

Vella Lavella

CHOISEUL

NEW GEORGIA

Rendova

SANTA ISABEL

Tulagi

GUADALCANAL

MALAITA

SAN CRISTOBAL

SOLOMON SEA

NEW GUINEA

Port Moresby

CORAL SEA

Introduction

The South Pacific Coast Watching Network

The idea for a coast watching network originated in the year 1919, beginning as a defensive measure to protect the long, and virtually unprotected, coastline of Australia. At that time, the country's population was concentrated primarily in the southeast section of the continent; in the event of war, an enemy could launch a surprise air attack on this area by crossing a wide expanse of desolate territory. To counter this threat, a plan was developed to use civilian spotters as coast watchers. They were equipped with telegraph and radio sets and were expected to act as an early warning system to report unidentified aircraft.

In September 1939, Lieutenant Commander Eric Feldt, Royal Australian Navy, was stationed at Port Moresby, New Guinea, and placed in charge of intelligence-gathering operations. The coast watching organization comprised about 800 people—the majority positioned along the Australian shore. A Solomon Islands screen, to the north, consisted of a few hundred plantation owners and managers. This group of spotters was spread very thin along the coasts of Buka, Bougainville, New Georgia, and other islands of the Solomon chain.

Lieutenant Commander Feldt gave his Solomon Islands watchers the code name FERDINAND, after the storybook character Ferdinand the bull, who preferred to sit under a tree and smell the flowers rather than fight. Although FERDINAND comprised a small group of spotters, its intelligence-gathering network covered more than a half million square miles of islands and ocean. Their nickname not only suited the members of this band of observers but also reminded them of their assignment as lookouts, not fighters. During World War II, however, there were many times when the Solomon Islands coast watchers, with their backs to the wall, were forced to battle the Japanese.

Prior to World War II, the Australian mandated islands of Buka and Bougainville comprised the Administrative District of Kieta, which was then part of the mandated territory of New Guinea.

Bougainville, 120 miles long and averaging 40 miles in width, was typical of the Solomon Islands chain—hostile jungles and rugged mountains, rising like flexed muscles from the serene sea. In late 1941, the population of Bougainville consisted of 70,000 natives. Also living on the island were 150 Europeans and Americans—including plantation workers and missionaries. About a hundred Chinese were engaged in commerce along the coast.

The small island of Buka is separated from the north end of Bougainville by a narrow strip of water known as the Buka Passage. Buka, 30 miles long and 10 miles wide, was home to 10,000 natives and several dozen Europeans.

For administrative purposes, the Bougainville area was divided into three districts—Buka Passage in the north, Kieta on the east coast, and Buin at the southern tip. Kieta was the main seat of government, while the small coral island of Sohano, in the strait that divided Buka and Bougainville, controlled the Passage. Kangu was the government station headquarters of the Buin district.

Industry in the islands consisted mainly of the production of copra, and the large native population became a fertile bartering ground for the Chinese traders. A small amount of gold mining was carried on in the central highlands, but scarcely on a profitable basis.

Jack Read entered the New Guinea public service in 1929 and acquired a firsthand intimate knowledge of the territory. In July 1941, he was appointed to the Buka Passage District on Sohano Island. Read's transfer to the Passage was also his introduction to the teleradio and its utilization.

The teleradio was a heavy and unwieldy radio and telegraph combination set. It was battery operated with a voice range of 400 miles and a range of about 600 miles when using the telegraph key. The device was sturdy and efficient, but because of its weight—plus batteries, charging engine, and benzine fuel—several men were required to carry the complete unit from one site to another.

By the time war came to the South Pacific on December 8, 1941, an excellent intradistrict communication network had been established on Bougainville. A daily radio schedule was maintained between the Buka Passage and various stations along the east coast of the island. This reporting system, put into effect by Lieutenant Commander Feldt, was destined to become the nucleus of coast watching activities on Bougainville for almost two years.

Paul Mason, who was a manager at the Inus Plantation on the east coast of Bougainville, was recruited as a volunteer coast watcher in 1939. However, his radio station was located four miles inland and was not ideally situated for coast watching purposes. Paul Mason therefore positioned native lookouts high in the hills, where they were able to view the coastline from Teop, in the north, to as far south as Kieta. Watchers were also assigned to Inus Point with instructions to notify the radio outpost by bicycle courier of any important sightings.

Lieutenant Commander Eric Feldt wrote:

So secret was this organization of coast watchers, operating behind enemy lines, that its existence was never admitted during the war. Few realized that when the first waves of United States Marines landed on the bitterly contested beaches of Guadalcanal, coast watchers on Bougainville, New Georgia, and other islands had been sending warning signals of impending Japanese air raids almost two hours before enemy aircraft formations appeared over the island.[1]

Japanese shipping was also spotted and telegraphed to Guadalcanal headquarters. This information was directly responsible for the U.S. victory in November 1942, when 12 Japanese transports, loaded with reinforcements, were intercepted and destroyed.

NOTE

1. Eric Feldt, *The Coast-Watchers*, (Melbourne: Oxford University Press, 1946).

CHAPTER 1

The Retreat from Buka Island and the Abandonment of Kieta

DECEMBER 12, 1941–AUGUST 7, 1942

Jack Read

On December 12, 1941, the Australian government ordered all European women and children evacuated from Bougainville. However, the order contained a stipulation: nurses and missionaries were given a choice as to whether they wished to remain on the island. Those few words of the proviso eventually created one of the biggest problems that the coast watchers were faced with on Bougainville, for the Sisters of the Marist Mission Society elected to stay.

Several plantation managers also refused to leave their homes. Mrs. Huson, of the Hanahan Plantation on Buka, decided to take her chances in case of Japanese attacks on the island. And on Bougainville, Mrs. E. Falkner at the Tearouki Plantation near Teop also rejected the government's directive. Mr. C. Campbell of the Raua Plantation had been very ill, and his wife refused to leave without him. The women were advised that if they remained on the island they would be doing so at their own risk. I later regretted that I had not taken the initiative and forcibly moved them aboard ship.

The people wishing to leave for Australia were notified to assemble at specified pick-up locations by the 18th. All the women and children in my district were informed to gather at the government district headquarters station at Sohano.

1

On December 17, the interisland schooner, *Asakaze*, cleared the Buka Passage en route from Rabaul, New Britain, to Kieta, on the east coast of Bougainville. The ship's captain had instructions to pick up evacuees waiting at Kieta, then head for Sohano Island to rescue the 13 adults and 4 children that I had assembled.

At dawn on the 19th, the *Asakaze* docked at Sohano and picked up my group of refugees. At seven o'clock, the ship sailed for Rabaul, and a short time later it ran into one of the most vicious tropical storms ever recorded in this area. There were no passenger accommodations on the small vessel—only blankets spread on the deck and hatches. The discomfort and terror of the people who made that voyage can be gauged by the fact that a normal crossing of 20 hours took twice as long to complete. The *Asakaze* finally reached Rabaul on the night of the 20th, and the shivering, water-soaked evacuees quickly scrambled aboard a transport leaving for Australia.

There was immediate criticism of the government's relief operation, deploring the fact that women and children were forced to travel on a beat-up old schooner with inadequate facilities.

I must admit that I was forced to concur somewhat with the bitter feelings expressed. Three weeks later, the steamer *Malaita* crossed the Passage heading south from Rabaul to Australia. On board this ship were more than 40 Japanese internees traveling with the luxury of a cabin and bunk, and waited upon by white stewards in the dining salon. This was certainly a great advertisement for Democracy and its principles—but not under these circumstances.

Throughout this period, a 24-hour vigil was maintained on the teleradio network. A so-called "X" frequency had been developed, which afforded a continuous open channel for sending any urgent coast watching reports. My orders were to use the "X" frequency to transmit important messages—such as the sighting of unidentified shipping and aircraft—to Lieutenant Commander Hugh Mackenzie at Station VIJ Rabaul. Beyond carrying out a few test calls, I had no cause to use the emergency channel until January 1942, when the Japanese thrust began to menace New Guinea and enemy reconnaissance planes first appeared over the Buka Passage.

The previous September, a 1,400-foot airstrip had been completed on Buka Island, and a detachment of AIF [Australian Imperial Force] under the command of Lieutenant J. M. Mackie was stationed at the field. Large quantities of gasoline, oil, and 250-pound bombs were stored in the vicinity. Mackie and the 25 men under his command were charged with the defense of the strip. In case of a heavy enemy attack, Corporal Bill Dolby was to mine the fuel and bomb depots. Machine guns were also posted alongside the airfield.

The situation was tenuous. Rabaul, Kavieng, and other cities in the territory were heavily bombed by unopposed Japanese aircraft, and there was disquieting news that a large enemy convoy was approaching Rabaul. Japanese scout planes were also appearing more frequently over Buka and Bougainville.

The Royal Australian Airforce was using Soraken as an intermediary refueling base for their Catalina flying boats. Usually a couple of these craft would drop down in the late afternoon, spend the night, and then take off at dawn on reconnaissance patrol.

Bomb and fuel dumps were established at Soraken, but the Japanese were evidently aware of the storage areas because the port came in for its share of bombing and strafing whenever enemy aircraft pounded the Buka Passage.

I became friendly with several members of the Catalina crews, and they were a cheery bunch of fellows—invariably a mixture of Americans and Australians—who bemoaned their inability to get a decent crack at the semiobsolete crates the Japanese were using over Rabaul simply because we had nothing with which to stop them. My real appreciation of the Cats, and the men who flew them, would come later in the darker months ahead.

Early on the morning of January 21, two Catalinas, which had remained overnight at Soraken, took off without their usual farewell and headed south. We regarded the sudden

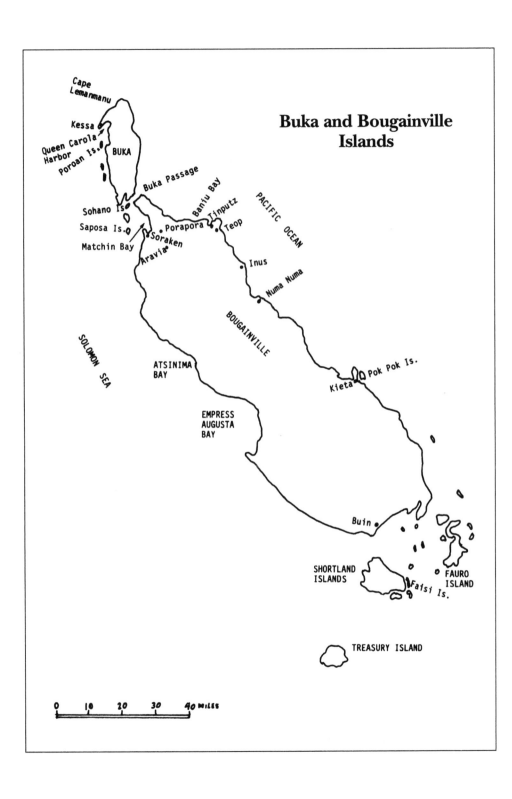

Buka and Bougainville Islands

Cape Lemanmanu

Kessa

Queen Carola Harbor
Poroan Is.

BUKA

Buka Passage

Baniu Bay

Sohano Is.

Tinputz

PACIFIC OCEAN

Saposa Is.

Porapora

Teop

Matchin Bay

Soraken

Aravia

Inus

Numa Numa

BOUGAINVILLE

SOLOMON SEA

ATSINIMA BAY

Pok Pok Is.

Kieta

EMPRESS AUGUSTA BAY

Buin

SHORTLAND ISLANDS

FAURO ISLAND

Faisi Is.

TREASURY ISLAND

0   10   20   30   40 MILES

departure as rather ominous. About noon, I received a signal that VIJ Rabaul was off the air and I should communicate any further reports to Station VIG Port Moresby, New Guinea. About the same time, a formation of Japanese flying boats appeared from the northwest. They slowly circled the Passage at a high altitude, then continued on their original course.

The Allied position was deteriorating rapidly, and I decided to establish an emergency supply dump in case I had to move out in a hurry. I did not know the countryside very well, but on the advice of old-timers I transferred a quantity of hard rations and essential equipment to Aravia. The village was only a spot on the map to me, and I never realized how difficult it was to get there. In order to reach Aravia from the Passage, it was necessary to take a road down the east coast of Bougainville for about 20 miles to the Baniu Plantation, then travel inland and climb for nearly two hours to reach the settlement—more than a thousand feet above sea level.

Lieutenant Mackie, also with an eye to the future, set up a few scattered dumps in the hills behind Soraken—south of Aravia and inland from Raua Bay.

I urged all remaining Europeans to do the same. But many declined on the grounds that it would be detrimental to white prestige to give the natives any inkling that the Europeans might be forced to abandon the island. The Chinese community of the Buka Passage took a more practical approach, however. They prepared a getaway near Baniu Bay. In fact, they moved their women and children to the location several days before the passage suffered its first air raid.

Rabaul fell on January 23, 1942, and two days later Japanese reconnaissance planes were seen circling slowly over the Buka Passage, obviously making aerial surveys of the area. My intuition warned me that the Passage was next on the Emperor's list.

The very next day, an enemy flying boat flew across Buka Island at an altitude of only a few hundred feet. As the plane neared the airfield, Mackie and his men expected to be bombed or strafed—but nothing happened. The craft made a wide circle and came over the field again. This time the AIF gun crews opened fire, and a few fragments of fuselage floated down. The Japanese now knew that there was still opposition at the Passage.

I decided quickly that it was time to abandon my post at Sohano. All hands were put to work collecting our supplies and equipment in preparation for moving to a safer location. Native runners were dispatched to all European residents on Buka Island, informing them of my action and advising them to escape to Bougainville. Corporal Dolby was ordered to set off the explosive charges to the fuel and ammunition depots.

Throughout the night, all traffic from Sohano and Buka led across the strait to Bonis. I packed our valuable records and cash. Various other files, maps, and anything else that might be of value to the enemy was destroyed. I turned in about 3 A.M. to grab a few hours sleep before taking a government launch (the *Nugget*) to Baniu. I hoped to locate a suitable site in that area to set up shop.

About 7 A.M. I attempted to contact VIJ Rabaul and VIG Port Moresby—but no luck. I dismantled the teleradio, loaded it aboard the *Nugget*, and shoved off.

We reached Bonis an hour later. I decided to take the launch, along with a few native police boys, and head directly for Baniu. The rest of my men would wait for additional supplies to arrive from Sohano and then join me as soon as possible.

We were only under way about 15 minutes when a single-engine Japanese float plane flew over us at high altitude. My native crew and I watched anxiously as the aircraft circled our boat.

During moments like this your imagination plays tricks with the mind. Your own importance soars. You immediately visualize yourself as the all-important target. Such was my feeling until the plane disappeared into a cloud formation. But the sense of relief lasted only a few moments. Suddenly, the aircraft plunged out of the clouds and dived straight at us. There was no place to hide. I screamed for full speed. We crossed our fingers and prayed.

The Jap opened up with rapid bursts of machine-gun fire—bullets chewing a ragged path across the water. But we were in luck, he missed the *Nugget* by a couple of hundred yards.

The pilot must have been in a hurry. After his first sweep, he gave up the attack and headed northwest. Several minutes later, however, he reappeared—this time leading a formation of five large flying boats. But the squadron was not after small vessels. They were heading for Sohano. For the next half hour the enemy planes bombarded targets in the Passage area. Most of the bombs dropped harmlessly in the water, but four exploded on Sohano, demolishing the native hospital. Another bomb ripped the Buka airstrip, and one landed in the middle of the Chinese settlement near Bonis.

We reached Baniu without further mishap. However, after the incident with the float plane, I hugged the cliff-bound shore so close that the launch ran a real danger of piling up on the rocks. There is no safe place to land anywhere along that stretch of coastline. Since then, I have often thought that the Japanese pilots might not have been so easy on us if they had guessed the big part our teleradio was destined to play in their defeat at Guadalcanal.

The rest of my group, hauling supplies from Sohano, probably would not reach Baniu for another day. This delay gave me an opportunity to scout the vicinity. I took the launch and a few native police boys and planned to travel along the coast to Teop Harbor—partly to warn the residents of current events and also to pick up a bit of local knowledge.

Our first stop was the Marist Mission Station at Tinputz where I renewed my acquaintance with Bishop Thomas Wade and Father Albert Lebel. I carried on a long discussion with the Bishop and urged him to move his missionaries, especially the Sisters, away from the beach. Wade was a very worried man. He feared for his people in the event of a Japanese invasion, yet he could not conscientiously order them away from their post because that would be contrary to the tenets of his Church.

While I was at the mission, Brother Joseph arrived from Raua with disturbing news. Mrs. Campbell informed him that enemy forces had occupied Kieta; she had heard the announcement on radio from Australia. The District Officer, J. I. Merrylees, was reported to have abandoned the town.

The situation on Bougainville seemed to be worsening by the hour. I rounded up my crew and headed down the coast. At Teop, I met Doug Trotter who was about to return to his station at Baniu. I was also introduced to Mrs. Falkner and visited Reverend Alley, leader of the Methodist Mission on Teop Island. Alley advised me that he and Frank Burns, manager of the Teopasina Plantation, had already stashed a large quantity of provisions in the mountains behind the harbor.

The news about Kieta made no material difference to my plans, other than that I was in a hurry to reach Baniu without further delay and move our supplies to Aravia. Trotter agreed to accompany me on the return trip.

In the meantime, the rest of my men had arrived at Baniu. Upon hearing the rumor that Kieta was in enemy hands, they had already begun to move the stores [provisions and supplies] inland.

I concealed the *Nugget* in a small creek at the head of Baniu Bay and, with the help of several native carriers, hauled the teleradio to the new location. It was dusk when we reached Aravia. The following morning, I assembled the teleradio and sent a signal to Port Moresby relating the information of the raid on Buka Passage.

Sometime toward the end of January, my native scouts advised me that the Passage was still free of enemy troops. I also received a letter by runner from Drummond Thomson at Numa Numa. Thomson wrote that Kieta was definitely not occupied by the enemy. He stated that Merrylees, along with other European residents, had evacuated the town, and, after they had departed, the native population revolted and went on a looting rampage. Dr. Kroening [a local medical doctor] was finally able to establish order and assumed control. Thomson insisted that I go to Kieta and straighten out the mess. I immediately sent two of my assistants, Frank Green and Eric Guthrie, back to Sohano for more stores, while I took the launch to Kieta, arriving there the last day of January.

As we sailed into Kieta Harbor, I noticed a white flag flying from the government building. After we landed at Wong You's jetty, several native police boys appeared on the scene, including Sergeant Yauwika and Corporal Sali. Moments later Dr. Kroening arrived. I had not met the doctor before, but I was aware that he was a German alien and also the district medical officer. He had spent the last war interned in Australia, and he was known to be pro-Nazi.

I thanked Kroening for stepping into the breach left by Merrylees and informed the doctor that I had no intention of taking over from him. But, as Assistant District Officer, I did intend to carry on where Merrylees had left off. Kroening and I had no sooner finished our discussion than Sergeant Yauwika and his native police marched to the flagstaff and raised the Australian flag in place of the white surrender banner.

The story of what actually occurred at Kieta was responsible for the rumor that the town had been occupied by the Japanese, and it is a good example of the hysteria that existed at the beginning of the war:

On the morning of January 23, the Kieta wireless operator, H. Doherty, was unable to contact Sohano. For some unaccountable reason, a rumor then quickly spread that the Buka Passage had been bombed out. And that a Catalina flying boat had airlifted me to Australia.

About noon, police Corporal Abui, on duty at the high lookout post near the radio station above the town, spotted an enemy aircraft to seaward. He watched it disappear behind Pok Pok, the lofty island at the entrance to the harbor. The corporal nervously waited for the plane to reappear. However, because it seemed to be taking a rather long time to come into view, the police boy dispatched a native runner to the District Office to notify Merrylees. It takes a runner about ten minutes to reach Kieta from the outpost. But no sooner was the runner on his way than the plane showed up from behind the island. Corporal Abui immediately sent another man to inform Merrylees that the enemy aircraft had reappeared.

As soon as the first runner, out of breath and terror stricken, related the incident, the District Office erupted in a state of panic. Merrylees telephoned Doherty, ordering him to set fire to the radio station. Rumors began to fly all over the town—evacuation was the order of the day.

Undoubtedly under the impression that there was immediate danger and that a landing was being made, Merrylees commandeered Wong You's ketch, the *Herald*. The small boat was quickly packed with Europeans, including plantation managers, medical personnel, and missionaries. Varied and vivid were the stories told by reliable eyewitnesses of the arguing and jockeying for a place on the vessel. Latecomers were forced to leave their possessions ashore because of lack of space.

The general confusion became worse when the solitary plane that was responsible for all the commotion circled the area—obviously attracted by the blazing radio station. The *Herald* quickly left the dock, even though several Europeans had not yet jumped aboard. The stranded men hopped on bicycles and chased the ketch down the coast.

Midway between Kieta and Toimonapu, Merrylees and his evacuees came across Reverend Luxton, who was heading for Buin in his boat, the *Bilua*. Luxton's vessel was larger and more seaworthy than the *Herald*, and Merrylees persuaded the reverend to join the refugees. The Kieta gang transferred bag and baggage to the *Bilua*—sending Wong You's boat and its native crew back to Kieta.

The *Bilua*, with her load of evacuees, continued on to the Toimonapu Plantation where Merrylees located Tom Ebery, the plantation manager, and confiscated his teleradio equipment. Doherty then sent a message to Port Moresby stating that the Japs had landed at Kieta.

Ebery later informed Paul Mason how Merrylees and his group stayed at the plantation house that night and heard the Australian shortwave radio announce the enemy occupation of Kieta. It now seemed certain that the town was really seized—

until one of the men remarked, "Don't be silly, that's only what we told them!"

A suggestion was made that a few people bicycle back to Kieta and find out the truth, but nobody volunteered. So the next morning Luxton and his new-found friends returned to the ship. Speculation was rife on our end as to the reaction aboard the *Bilua* when, according to a local priest, a Japanese flying boat came down to masthead level for a closer look at the ship as it left port.

However, the humor of the incident was lost in the more serious side of the matter. As soon as Merrylees and his boat-load of refugees had sailed from Kieta, all hell broke loose in the town. The native residents were riled by the manner in which the Europeans had abandoned the city. Hundreds of natives from nearby villages flooded into Kieta and joined the local population in an orgy of looting and destruction. The natives smashed stores and laid waste to the contents. Sergeant Yauwika called out his police in a futile attempt to quell the riot. Dr. Kroening arrived on the scene just in time to prevent the mob from breaking into the liquor store. Although he was not popular with the police, due to his German nationality, Kroening managed to rally their aid and restore order.

About a week later, two Japanese planes flew over the town and dropped a couple of bombs. They fell harmlessly in the mission plantation nearly three miles from the city. It was the first show of enemy hostility against Kieta. Presumably the Japanese High Command had heard the broadcast and knew it to be false, but, nevertheless, they thought they had better do something about it.

Despite the pandemonium created by Merrylees, I realized that the fall of Kieta was only a matter of time. I immediately began to establish hidden supply dumps and cleared the town of anything that might prove valuable to the enemy. The bulk of the consumable provisions, which had been carted off to various villages during the looting, were gradually returned by the natives.

Using the *Herald* and another vessel, the *Malaguna,* I transported several tons of rice and other hard rations to principal locations up and down the coast. From these points the police worked incessantly, supervising transfer of the supplies into the mountains. These dumps eventually proved to be a godsend.

But we had not heard the last of Merrylees and his "merry men." Within a fortnight, another announcement was received from Australia. It seems that Merrylees and his entourage had crossed the Solomon Sea and reached Port Moresby. The broadcast was an elaborate story of the District Officer's feat in navigating the *Bilua* across the ocean without instruments. Merrylees reported his timely evacuation of all Europeans—and fantastically described Kieta as having been captured by two enemy airmen who planted the Japanese flag. He also stated that before the town was abandoned he had set fire to the office and destroyed all records.

The fallacy of this account can be judged by the fact that the actual occupation of Kieta did not take place until July 1942. And that no attempt was made to destroy anything in the District Office—I did that myself before finally leaving Kieta to its fate.

CHAPTER 2

Organizing the Coast Watching Operation in Northern Bougainville

FEBRUARY 20–APRIL 5, 1942

Jack Read

On February 20, I put Sergeant Yauwika in charge at Kieta and returned to the Buka Passage on the *Malaguna*. During my absence, Eric Guthrie and Frank Green had organized gangs of native labor and moved large quantities of provisions from Sohano to Aravia. And Lieutenant Mackie shifted his location to Matahai in the Ramasan Valley.

A few days later I was back aboard the *Malaguna* for the return trip to Kieta. We stopped at plantations on our way south, picking up district officers and anyone else who wished to escape the Japanese threat. Once again, I tried to convince the Campbells, Mrs. Huson, Mrs. Falkner, and the Marist Sisters to leave the island, but none of them would budge.

I reached Inus on the 24th and met with Paul Mason and Drummond Thomson. Paul and I were notified of our appointment as sergeants in the New Guinea Administrative Unit. Mason also had received two messages from Lieutenant Commander Feldt. They read in part:

> You will be of great value if you can remain and keep contact for over six months. Suggest you prepare a base two days inland and retire to it when necessary. Make a

13

garden and stock up with fowl and pigs. If you want essential spares and stores, advise your requirements and we may be able to drop them.

Paul Mason and I both accepted the challenge and sent a reply to that effect.

The *Malaguna* docked at Kieta on the 26th. I blew open the District Office safe—took cash and other valuables and packed them for transfer to Aravia. That afternoon, the last official mail was placed aboard a ship heading for Tulagi in the southern Solomons. Also bundled aboard the vessel were the record books and important papers that were alleged to have been destroyed by Merrylees. Frank Green and Doug Trotter were among the group that left for Tulagi.

Besides myself and Paul Mason, a few other government officials elected to remain—Drummond Thomson, Wallace Brown, Fred Archer, and Percy Good. I think they were more or less influenced by my decision not to leave the island. At dusk we all boarded the *Malaguna* and sailed northward from Kieta.

A survey of our position, as I saw it, revealed that our specific task on Bougainville would be coast watching. We had ample teleradio equipment on hand and the manpower to run it. In conference with Lieutenant Mackie, it was decided to pool our resources and to establish coast watching posts with the approval of Lieutenant Commander Feldt.

Five stations were set up. They were composed of AIF personnel, native police, and radio operators. Station call signals were assigned, transmission schedules were planned, and provision arrangements were made.

A teleradio outpost was established at Kessa on Cape Lemanmanu to cover northern Buka Island, using the call letters XYZ, and it was commanded by Signalman D. L. Sly. Corporal Dolby at station KLM, Numa Numa, blanketed the center of the east coast of Bougainville. The Inus location was set up to overlook Kieta Harbor and was handled by Paul Mason at station GHI. The Buin-Faisi area was positioned at Kangu and was assigned the call letters DMK. I established my post overlooking the Buka Passage using my initials, WJR, as the signal code.

The undertaking was not easy. Nevertheless, the plan was fully operational by March 6, 1942. I felt that we had Bougainville effectively covered, and it was merely a matter of sitting back and waiting for things to happen. Our outside contact was Lieutenant Macfarlan at station VNTG Tulagi. That station kept an around-the-clock watch, and our communication was always at maximum signal strength.

The balance of Army personnel, not directly engaged in coast watching, was split into two sections. One party, under Corporal D. M. McLean, was stationed at Matahai, while the other group, commanded by Corporal Harry Cameron, was camped at Sorem Village near the Passage.

Eric Guthrie remained at Bonis, supervising the transfer of supplies from Sohano to Aravia. I was busy trying to locate a more suitable base farther inland.

Lieutenant Mackie was dispatched to Buin with a coast watching team. En route he stopped at Kieta and arrested Dr. Kroening. We did not trust the German and wanted him out of the way. A transport, the *Ruana*, met Mackie at Buin with a shipload of supplies and then sailed for Tulagi with the German doctor and his wife on board. Drummond Thomson and Wallace Brown also decided to head south on the *Ruana*.

At various times during the next couple of days, both Paul Mason and I heard XYZ calling from Kessa, but we were unable to establish communications. Then, on the morning of March 9, we heard XYZ calling WJR with an urgent signal to deliver. We were still unable to make contact, and, apprehensive as to what the message could be, I dispatched a native runner from Aravia to Cape Lemanmanu—a three-day journey.

Late Wednesday, March 11, I heard from Fred Archer at his plantation on the west coast of Buka. He reported that six Japanese cruisers and two destroyers had anchored at Queen Carola Harbor on the previous Monday. This was obviously the urgent message that XYZ was trying to transmit. I immediately passed the information on to VNTG Tulagi.

I was disappointed at the failure of XYZ to cope with the situation. Evidently Signalman Sly was not sufficiently instructed in the operation of the radio. I decided to move closer to the Passage and try to remedy the problem with my own equipment. On Thursday morning I received further word from Archer that the enemy ships had put to sea Tuesday night. I sent the latest information to VNTG and proceeded to the Buka Passage. When I reached Sorem I met the group that had been manning Station XYZ and heard their version of what had occurred at Kessa.

Signalman Sly stated that on Monday morning his lookouts at Cape Lemanmanu sighted Japanese ships at about eight miles and bearing on a course for Queen Carola Harbor. However, because he was unfamiliar with the radio transmitter he was not able to send the message. A few hours later the coast watchers were almost surprised by an enemy landing party. Sly and his men barely had time to dismantle the teleradio and hide it in the jungle brush.

Father Hennessy, an American priest in charge of the local mission, intercepted the Japanese patrol, thereby giving the watchers a chance to escape. An enemy officer questioned Hennessy about the location of English soldiers and teleradios. But language difficulties, plus a bit of deliberate procrastination, helped the priest keep out of trouble—and at the same time avoid divulging any useful information.

Hennessy was placed on parole and ordered not to leave the mission or communicate with anyone. After the Japanese scouting party returned to their ship, the XYZ team hightailed it to Sorem—but they did not take the teleradio with them. I sent a native police party back to Cape Lemanmanu to retrieve the radio. Then I hurried to the Bonis Plantation, where I met with the manager, Alf Long. Eric Guthrie and Fred Archer joined us there.

Archer informed me that Percy Good, at the Kessa Plantation, had also been visited by the Japanese. When the enemy patrol inspected his house, the ground floor of the building looked like a radio repair shop. Good admitted to them that at one time he did operate a teleradio, but not recently. Percy was placed on parole and watched carefully.

On March 13, Australian broadcast stations announced the presence of a Japanese naval force at Queen Carola Harbor. My message to Tulagi had been the basis for the story. The news broadcast confirmed enemy suspicions that a teleradio was operating on Buka. It was distressingly evident to us that coast watching was not going to enjoy much of a future under these circumstances. Fortunately the uncensored announcements did not continue.

However, Percy Good was now in real danger. He had to be brought to Bougainville as soon as possible. The Japanese had buoyed the harbor. They would be returning, and Percy had to be prevented from further contact with the enemy—for his own protection as well as ours.

On the assumption that a show of force might be necessary, I organized an armed expedition to leave immediately for Kessa. Besides myself, other members of the party included Eric Guthrie, Fred Archer, Alf Long, Harry Cameron, Signalman Sly, Brother Joseph, and a few native police.

This was Sunday, March 15. We were about to shove off in the *Nugget* when a native scout brought news that the warships had just returned to Kessa. There was no alternative but to call off the expedition until the coast was clear—and to trust that all would go well with Percy Good.

On Wednesday, March 18, Police Constable Owanda brought word that the ships had put to sea Monday night—and that Percy had been killed and buried near his house.

By midnight on the 18th we were underway in the *Nugget*, and by dawn we had docked at the Methodist Mission at Skotolan. Not relishing the risk of crossing Queen Carola Harbor by daylight in a motor launch, we transferred to canoes and reached Kessa about noon.

Local natives directed us to Percy's grave in a small garden plot on the south side of his bungalow. Corporal Sali supervised the exhumation of the body while I checked the house. In the hallway there was a large pool of dried blood, along with

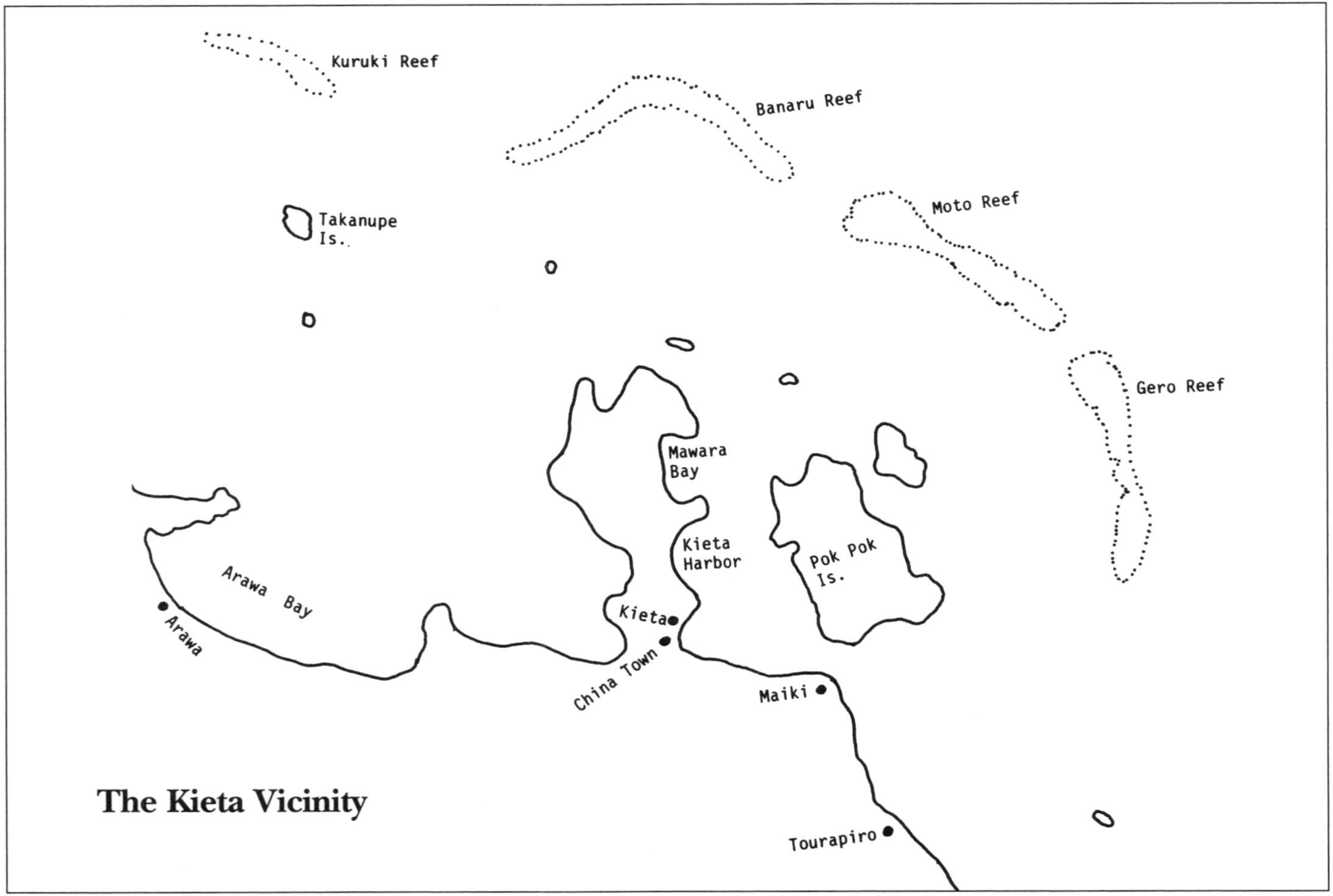
The Kieta Vicinity
Kuruki Reef
Banaru Reef
Moto Reef
Gero Reef
Takanupe Is.
Mawara Bay
Kieta Harbor
Pok Pok Is.
Arawa Bay
Arawa
Kieta
China Town
Maiki
Tourapiro

blood-stained footprints of small pointed rubber-soled sandals—like those worn by Japanese sailors.

Within a few minutes, Sali reported that the body had been uncovered, and I joined the others at the grave side. The corpse was confirmed to be that of Percy Good. A close examination revealed that a bullet had entered through the left ear and exited just above the right eye. His jaw was broken, and there were other marks and abrasions about the face and neck.

We stood trancelike—shocked and angered. There was a strained silence: not a word was spoken as the body was reburied in its shallow grave. Only the roar of the Pacific as it crashed violently against the coral, reef-bound shore behind us broke the quiet. Suddenly a flying boat droned low over the tall palms of Kessa, and I noticed the dull red disk on its fuselage. My only thought at that moment was that Percy Good, the first of our number to fall victim to Japanese barbarism, would someday be avenged.

We launched our canoes at sunset and headed for Skotolan. In the last light of day I spotted two destroyers a few miles to seaward. While waiting for the moon to appear, we stopped at Poroan Island and made a meal of bully beef, biscuits, and tea. A crowd of natives gathered around us. I spoke to them along propaganda lines, but they were as apprehensive about the future as we were. And who could blame them? The Japanese had consolidated their base at Rabaul. Singapore had fallen, and the American position in the Philippines was tenuous. Our home shores at Darwin had been raided, and the enemy was nibbling at the Solomon Islands. Bougainville began to loom even larger as the next meal on the Emperor's journey.

As we traveled cautiously across the water from Poroan to Skotolan, I resolved to chase the remaining Europeans out of Buka. The incident at Kessa did not augur well for anyone falling into Japanese hands.

The Hanahan Plantation was located between Skotolan and the Buka Passage. I stopped at Mrs. Huson's home near the plantation, and, after much arguing, I finally convinced her to come with us. We also evacuated four American Sisters at a mission in the northeastern part of the island. The *Nugget* transported them all to Tinputz. If they had remained at their stations another week, Mrs. Huson and the Sisters would have been hopelessly cut off by the imminent Japanese occupation of the Passage.

I reorganized the XYZ station team and posted them at a high vantage point near Skotolan. From this location they commanded a full view of Queen Carola Harbor and everything west of Buka. The group comprised Corporal Cameron, Signalman Sly, and three police boys. They were on the job by March 22, and I planned to check on them in a few days. Meanwhile, the other stations—GHI, KLM, and DMK—were functioning perfectly, even though, at this stage of the game, there was not much to report except an occasional enemy aircraft flying southeast.

During the last week of March, Lieutenant Mackie joined me at the Passage, leaving Corporal McLean in charge of shifting their supplies from Buin to the Army base at Matahai.

All aspects of our operation seemed to be going well. We had an efficient network of coast watchers covering strategic points on the island. My only concern was the remaining civilian white population. They steadfastly refused to take the future seriously—and they were generally imbued with the idea, the hope, that the planters would still be free to produce copra and the missionaries would be permitted to carry on with their religious duties—even under Japanese occupation.

As a coast watcher, my interest in the civilians was mainly the fact that, if they fell into enemy hands, they might, under duress, divulge vital information about our activities.

On March 27, Mackie and I returned to Skotolan with the *Nugget.* Station XYZ was now operating smoothly. We left at dusk on the 29th and reached Bonis at midnight. I had planned to take the launch down the coast to Baniu on the following evening, then conceal it in a creek and join Guthrie at Aravia. To fill in the time, pending my departure for Baniu, I decided to take the *Nugget* on a scouting trip around the tiny islands off

Soraken. Corporal Sali and I, along with two native crewman, shoved off about two in the morning. By dawn on March 30, we were approaching Hog Island.

Although it did not mean much to me at the time, I remember sighting the smoke of ships on the western horizon. We continued on to the Sopio Mission where I met Father Herbert. We talked for a few hours, and I picked up a great deal of local information that proved valuable to me at a later date.

The journey was taking longer than anticipated, and it was about nine o'clock that night when we reached Soraken Point. From there I headed straight across Matchin Bay. We were within a couple of miles of Sohano when Corporal Sali reported seeing a large ship ahead that was hugging the coast. Neither the crew nor I noticed anything unusual, so we continued on course. A few minutes later, Sali insisted that there was definitely a vessel hiding along the shore. My maxim has always been to play safe. I ordered the engine cut off. We drifted in silent uncertainty for a minute. Then, just as I was about to have the motor restarted, I heard the high revving sound of another engine coming our way. We lost no time in putting the launch about and headed for Soraken at top speed. I was thankful that the *Nugget* was a silent running job.

We stopped our motor several times to ascertain if we were being followed, but the stranger's engine noise soon died away.

I spotted a fire burning on a small island near the coast, and the crew cautiously maneuvered the launch through a maze of reefs to the atoll. Constable Lunga met us at the landing. He told me that the Japanese had occupied the Buka Passage and that he and Corporal Auna had been detailed to patrol duty in the Soraken area.

According to Lunga, just after daybreak a Japanese cruiser stood off the western end of the Passage and shelled Sohano, while an aircraft flew over and dropped a few bombs on the island. Shortly afterward, two destroyers and a transport entered the anchorage. Throughout the day Japanese troops landed at Soraken and other points in the Passage. The ships were still at anchor by nightfall.

We had almost sailed into a pack of trouble. My plan now was to conceal the *Nugget* and still find a way to reach the mainland of Bougainville before daybreak. The fuel tank of the launch was nearly empty, which precluded sending it down the west coast to find a suitable hiding place. I hesitated to destroy the craft and had the crew tow the boat by canoe to a stream near the head of Matchin Bay. Corporal Sali and I jumped in another canoe and headed for Porton.

We paddled cautiously as we had no knowledge as to whether the Japanese landing parties had returned to their ships. When we reached the village, it appeared deserted. Not taking any chances, we cut across a mangrove swamp toward the Marist Mission Training Center at Chabai. It was still dark, and, fearing that there might be enemy soldiers at the mission, I deemed it wise to wait until daylight before proceeding.

I tried to keep my mind off the millions of mosquitoes that swarmed over us in the swamp by wondering how the XYZ team was making out—and by reflecting on our future.

Dawn found Chabai all clear. The Brothers, who ran the center, had escaped into the bush when the Japs landed. We helped ourselves to their provisions and made breakfast. I hope to meet up with the Brothers someday and thank them for that welcome morning meal made at their expense.

I carefully scouted the coast as we continued on toward the Tarlena Mission. I soon sighted a transport and a destroyer anchored near Taiof Island and observed numerous small craft plying cargo to Sohano.

When we reached Tarlena, I met Father McConville, Father Morelle, and three Sisters. Laurie Chan, the Australian-educated Chinese storekeeper, had also taken refuge in the mission with his wife and family.

We sat down to an appetizing dinner prepared by the women. However, while eating, I kept nervously looking seaward. Suddenly an enemy schooner emerged from behind Sohano. The ship gave the impression of sailing for Soraken. But, when it was directly opposite Tarlena, the vessel changed course and swung sharply for our location.

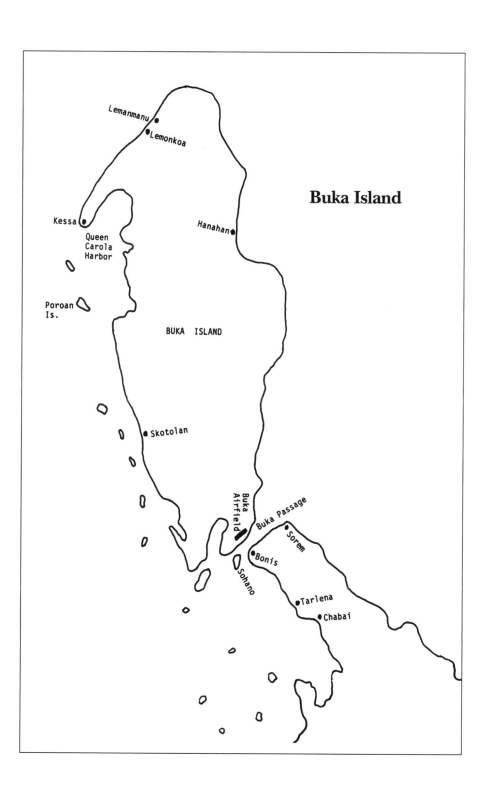

Lemanmanu

Lemonkoa

Buka Island

Kessa

Hanahan

Queen
Carola
Harbor

Poroan
Is.

BUKA ISLAND

Skotolan

Buka
Airfield

Buka Passage

Sorem

Bonis

Sohano

Tarlena

Chabai

Fathers McConville and Morelle hurried to hide the Sisters and the Chan family in the jungle. I turned my binoculars on the schooner and noted it carried a machine gun both fore and aft. About 20 soldiers were standing amidships. The ship was only a few hundred yards from the jetty when the guns began spraying the shore.

I figured that this was the time to beat a hasty retreat. Sali and I joined the missionaries at their temporary hideout a quarter mile or so from the mission. But the Japanese were only interested in looting. They filled the schooner with clothing, stores and livestock. And, in about an hour, they headed back to Sohano.

We returned to the beach and viewed the damage. However, I was anxious to be on my way and urged the missionaries to leave for Aravia where I could supply them with rations. But my pleading was in vain, so I bid them farewell and took the trail to the east coast. McConville, Morelle, and the Sisters were eventually captured by the Japanese, but they were not treated harshly. As for Laurie Chan and his family, they became victims of circumstances. Mrs. Chan was pregnant, and it was necessary that she remain under the care of the Tarlena Sisters—otherwise they would have escaped to Baniu with the rest of the Chinese community.

The Japanese immediately commandeered Laurie's services as an interpreter, and he became a virtual prisoner at Sohano. Public opinion, in all its ignorance, branded him a traitor. In actual fact, Chan continually passed valuable information to us by way of Father McConville. During the time Laurie Chan was kept captive at the Passage, rumor has it that his wife was forced to live with a Japanese officer.

Late in the afternoon, after leaving Tarlena, we spotted Corporal Auna. I mistakenly believed he would be the perfect person to deliver a message to Station XYZ—informing the coast watchers of what was happening at the Passage. I had learned that native traffic across to Buka was barred, but Auna was certain he could reach Skotolan. I scribbled a noncommittal note to Lieutenant Mackie and sent the fellow on his way.

That was the last I ever saw of Auna—even his countrymen disowned the police boy—and he was a dead man if I ever caught up with him.

Auna did manage to deliver the message to the coast watchers, but then he reported it to the Japanese and led an enemy patrol in pursuit of the XYZ party.

Mackie and his men barely managed to elude the Japs, and they finally escaped across the passage about mid-April. But before going off the air and fleeing the enemy, the coast watchers sent a last-second dispatch to Station VNTG reporting that five Japanese cruisers and destroyers had entered Queen Carola Harbor.

As Corporal Sali and I made our way east, we were hailed by Sergeant Waramabi. He had anticipated our route to Aravia and had posted native police along the trail to give warning of any enemy patrols. I was informed that Fred Archer and the Army personnel at Sorem had withdrawn to Baniu.

At Waramabi's suggestion, we deviated from the main trail in order to get a close view of Sohano. Under cover of a mangrove field, at the western end of the Bonis Plantation, I was able to sneak near enough to observe the activity around that area of the Passage. I sighted a destroyer at anchor and observed two schooners disembark about a hundred soldiers at Sohano. The entire vicinity was a beehive of activity. I had no doubt that this was a permanent Japanese occupation force.

There was nothing more to do or see around the Passage, so we set out on the 20-mile journey to Baniu and inland to Aravia. By dusk I had reached a small village atop a cliff overlooking the sea. I noticed two heavy cruisers steaming slowly toward the Passage. I was told by the natives that more warships had been seen during the day.

It was dark by the time we reached Baniu, and I was surprised to find Alf Long. He had arrived aboard the *Malaguna*, which was tied up at the wharf. We had previously discussed the possibility of sending the Chinese refugees at Baniu farther south to Numa Numa. There were a large number of children involved, and it would be a more satisfactory arrangement. So, on the previous night, Long had carefully dodged Japanese warships and sneaked the *Malaguna* into Baniu to rescue the Chinese. He intended to sail at midnight in order to make Numa Numa by daybreak. I was not keen on the project with so much enemy shipping about. And, although we did not know it at the time, a Japanese destroyer was anchored only a few miles away.

However, any decision was a gamble at this time, and Alf Long was prepared to take the risk. He put to sea at midnight with his Chinese passengers. They arrived at Numa Numa safely and survived a year of extreme privation and hardships before eventually reaching Australia.

We spent the rest of the night in a native hut, and Fred Archer joined us at dawn the next day. Our small party then proceeded along the trail to Aravia. A new improved base had been established five miles farther inland. This location was useless for coast watching. And, in fact, my only consideration for selecting the spot was from the safety point of view. We had yet to learn how the Japanese would react—whether or not they would come after us.

The teleradio was operating on schedule, but I was unable to raise VIG Port Moresby. However, I had no difficulty in sending my messages through VNTG Tulagi, or by coast watcher C. L. Page, who was located somewhere in New Ireland.

Our own internal network had come up to expectations. Near the end of March, Station DMK signaled the first appearance of Japanese shipping in the Buin-Faisi area. We also received an urgent message from Station GHI reporting that two enemy cruisers and a transport had sent raiding parties ashore at Kieta.

On March 31, a Japanese destroyer anchored in Tinputz Harbor, and a military force went ashore at the mission station. Father Lebel, an actor if there ever was one, put on a first-class show for the enemy. As soon as the destroyer was sighted, Lebel sent the Sisters to a hideaway. Then, to create an impressive atmosphere, he donned his ecclesiastical robes and swaggered down to the beach.

The landing party was under the command of a young sub-lieutenant. The officer attempted to act like an educated gentleman, but he was embarrassed by his poor knowledge of the English language. The perturbed fellow fumbled with a Japanese-English dictionary and tried laboriously to communicate. He asked the usual and obvious questions. And the answers, though evasive, were accepted. The officer seemed completely satisfied with the response. Father Lebel felt very pleased with himself—the Jap probably did not understand a word that was being said to him.

The priest was therefore surprised when he was forced to accompany the sub-lieutenant back to the destroyer. Lebel was escorted into the ship's wardroom. Five naval officers seated in the compartment stood up and bowed respectfully. After answering more questions of no special importance, Father Lebel was told that he could return ashore and carry on his religious duties, but he had to promise that he would not leave the mission. The priest protested, saying that in order to continue his work, he must have the right to visit among his native flock. When asked which people were involved, he gave his reply in the form of a sweeping gesture across a map of Bougainville on the table in front of him. Whereupon Father Lebel's parole was amended to the effect that he must not leave the island. Hence his freedom to travel anywhere as long as he remained on Bougainville—and to visit me, which he did often in the months to come.

One interesting fact revealed to Lebel by the Japanese was their knowledge of the 25 Australian soldiers on the island. This figure, in fact, was the exact AIF strength.

Leaving Tinputz, the destroyer proceeded down the coast to Teop Harbor. At this time, Mrs. Huson was staying with Mrs. Falkner at the Tearouki Plantation near Teop. And Fred Urban, manager of the Hakau Coffee Estates, was visiting with Reverend Alley at the Methodist Mission.

When the enemy vessel appeared in the harbor, Urban and Alley decided to meet the landing party rather than try to escape, which would have left the women unprotected. How-

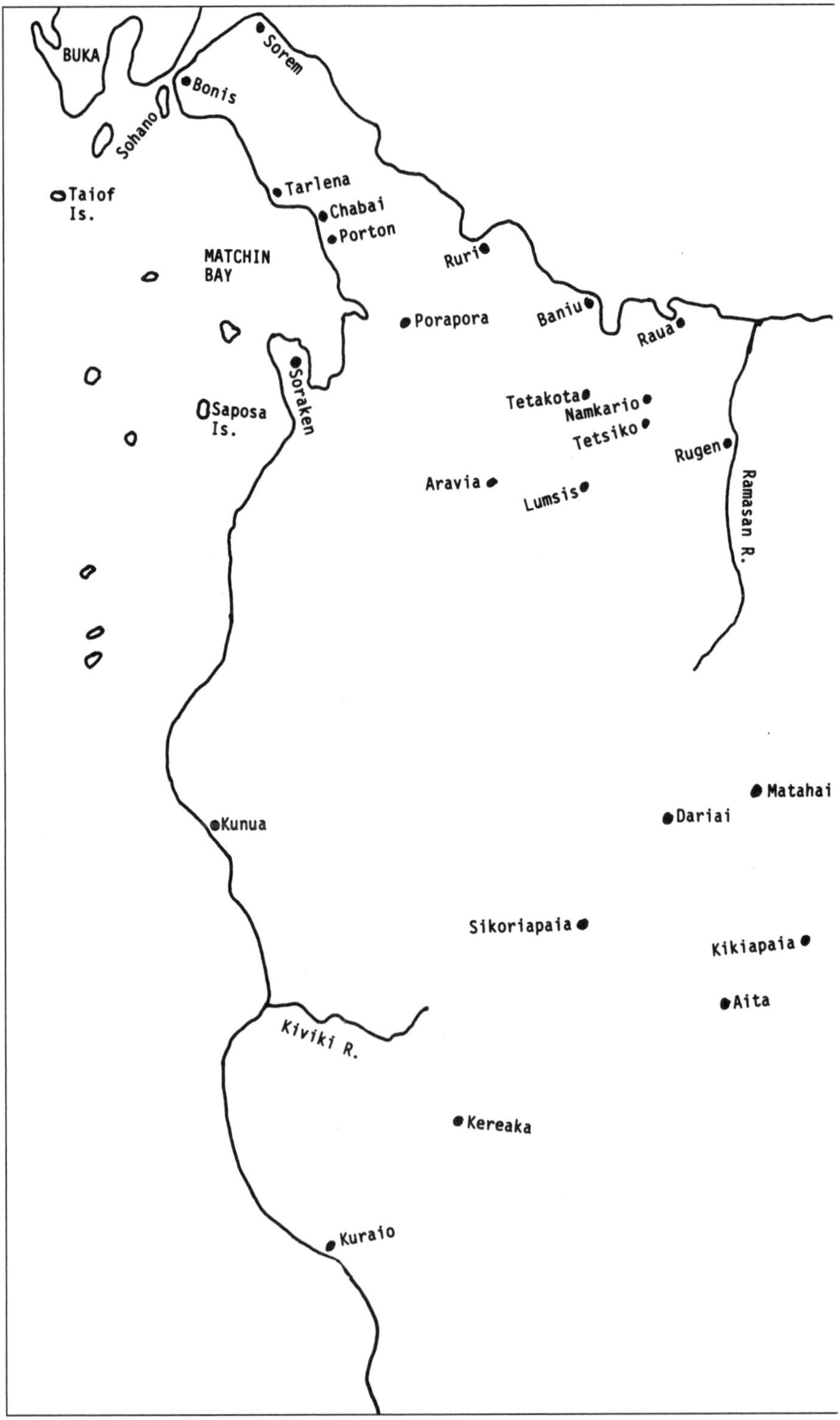
BUKA
Sohano
Bonis
Sorem
Taiof Is.
Tarlena
Chabai
Porton
MATCHIN BAY
Ruri
Porapora
Baniu
Raua
Soraken
Saposa Is.
Tetakota
Namkario
Tetsiko
Rugen
Aravia
Lumsis
Ramasan R.
Matahai
Dariai
Kunua
Sikoriapaia
Kikiapaia
Aita
Kiviki R.
Kereaka
Kuraio

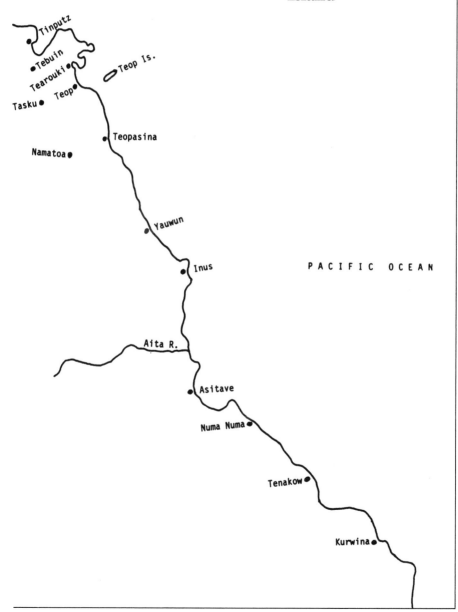

Northern Bougainville Island

Tinputz

Tebuin

Tearouki

Teop Is.

Tasku

Teop

Teopasina

Namatoa

Yauwun

Inus

PACIFIC OCEAN

Aita R.

Asitave

Numa Numa

Tenakow

Kurwina

ever, while the two men were delivered to the destroyer by one group of sailors, another detachment was sent to the plantation to question the women.

Fred Urban and Reverend Alley were detained on deck to await the destroyer's commanding officer. Urban happened to be leaning nonchalantly against the ship's railing when the captain approached. The officer flew into a rage, angrily rebuking Urban for not standing at attention and kicking him severely.

When asked his nationality, Fred replied that he was Austrian-born. However, the Jap captain, not well versed in English, thought Urban said Australian. The potentially dangerous misunderstanding was quickly corrected when Fred pointed to Austria on a map.

Reverend Alley stated that he was a New Zealander and was aware that a state of war existed between his country and Japan. The reverend's fate was decided quickly—he was to be interned. Alley was escorted back to the mission, where he packed his personal belongings, and then he returned to the destroyer.

Fred Urban remarked that the Japanese appeared to be concerned for the two women living alone at the Tearouki Plantation without protection. He credited this demeanor for the fact that he was allowed to remain on the island. However, he was warned not to leave the area or to do anything damaging to the Japanese cause. The destroyer sailed with Reverend Alley as a prisoner—and one wonders if we shall ever hear his version of what actually took place that day.

Neither Mrs. Huson nor Mrs. Falkner suffered any harsh treatment from the enemy. The Japanese merely intruded upon their privacy—learned nothing of value—confiscated a few items in the house, and then withdrew.

Regarding the courteous treatment accorded some of the missionaries and other Europeans, it must be remembered that, at this stage of the war, the Japanese were advancing southward without opposition, and they could well afford to be chivalrous.

I was commissioned with the rank of lieutenant in the Royal Australian Naval Volunteer Reserve on April 2, 1942, and Paul Mason was appointed a petty officer.

On April 5, Station DMK at Buin went off the air. The coast watchers were routed by a surprise enemy landing at Kangu. Mason, at Kieta, had been in contact with the outpost and had given the men several days warning of a possible enemy attack. Had the DMK party been on the alert, they could have escaped with their valuable equipment. As it was, they only had time to destroy the teleradio and flee into the jungle. They later joined Mason at Daratui.

Paul Mason knew the waters of the Buin-Faisi area better than most natives. He had lived in the Shortland Islands as a youngster and was very familiar with the region. Mason contacted Lieutenant Commander Feldt and received permission to move his coast watching operation to Buin. Paul might have foreseen the future development of the area under enemy occupation—and the possibilities of the intelligence job to be done there.

CHAPTER 3

Coast Watching Activities Begin in Earnest

APRIL 19–AUGUST 7, 1942

Jack Read

When Lieutenant Mackie reached Bougainville about the middle of April, he related the story of his coast watching team's escape from Buka.

Upon learning that enemy patrols were moving his way, Mackie signaled the presence of Japanese warships in Queen Carola Harbor and then shut down the station.

Friendly Fijian natives, led by Usaia Sotutu, hid the AIF men from Japanese search parties. Usaia knew every inch of Buka Island and guided the soldiers to the western end of the Passage. For several days, the Fijians kept the Army lads concealed until Usaia was able to find a few canoes. Then under cover of night, he sneaked the coast watchers and their teleradio across the Passage to Soraken.

It was imperative that I find another location for Station XYZ—and quickly. I decided to post Mackie and his men in the highlands directly behind the Inus Plantation. From that spot, they had a sweeping coverage of the Bougainville east coast from Buka almost to Kieta.

During the month of April 1942, the Japanese position in our area could be summed up as follows: Buka Passage was the only point of occupation, although several spasmodic landings had been made by raiding parties. Aerial flights by single-engine aircraft from northwest to southeast and return were increasing, and shipping activity heading south was becoming more noticeable. Enemy troop concentrations were reinforced by several hundred. But, by the end of the month, most of these had moved out, presumably for the attack and occupation of Tulagi.

Only a small garrison of about 50 men was left at Sohano. As far as our status was concerned, the Japs had not yet made any effort to come after us—although their threats to do so were rampant.

The native people of Buka and the villages on the Bougainville mainland adjacent to the Passage turned pro-Japanese immediately after their subjugation by the enemy. I do not think they did so from sheer disloyalty, because the New Guinea native has no appreciation of what the term means. His is still the primitive mind that responds to the more tangible things of life. He is attracted to anything novel—and particularly favors the hunter rather than the hunted. The incoming Japanese were all of the former, while we were the latter. Consequently, according to native perception, the Japs had prevailed. The people of the Passage had watched the Europeans flee, and they saw the hitherto respected white missionaries captured and imprisoned at Sohano. What was more natural for the primitive mind than to believe the enemy's stories claiming universal victory?

The first audacious stroke by the natives against us was the murder of Sergeant Waramabi. On April 19, Waramabi and Corporal Sanei were supervising the transfer of the last of our stores to Aravia. Waramabi discovered that several bags of rice were missing—and obviously had been stolen by the native carriers. During the course of questioning, both police boys were attacked by men armed with axes and knives. Sergeant Waramabi was killed outright, but Sanei, although badly wounded, managed to escape.

Fortunately, for the time being at least, we were able to keep the native pro-Japanese trend confined to the Buka Passage. Propaganda was our best weapon—plus my presence around Aravia. My influence lay solely in a general native respect for my former position as District Officer. The people were still not ready to betray me or my police.

The native communities remote from Japanese contact were not particularly interested in the new regime. They were content to continue bringing their various tribal and domestic disputes to me, relying on my inquiry and judgment. They also depended on our constant market for their produce—and we had the means to pay for every service rendered. Government funds amounting to about a thousand pounds had been saved from the district offices at Buka and Kieta. This money, plus trade goods such as tobacco and calico, enabled us to maintain an advantageous relationship with the population.

The Japanese themselves were a great help to us—had they known it. The enemy's method of commandeering labor, produce, and women without payment soon became annoying to the natives.

I continued to search the hill country for a coast watching site that would offer a clear, unclouded view overlooking the Passage. I spent a week in the Ramasan Valley near the Army base at Matahai. Lieutenant Mackie had been sending out small patrol parties to gather local information. But now most of his men were down sick with the usual ailments common among newcomers to the tropics—such as malaria, ulcerations, and scrub itch.

I arranged to leave my surplus supplies and gear at the Army base, while I scouted the high uninhabited mountain ranges near the Passage. On May 4, I located a site that afforded a panoramic view of Matchin Bay and Queen Carola Harbor. However, because of its high altitude—4,000 feet above sea level—the location would often be clouded in. But the spot could serve as a makeshift setup until I found something better.

About this time, I heard the astonishing news that Frank Burns had voluntarily surrendered to the enemy garrison at Sohano. He was living with Fred Urban at the Hakau Estates. While at Hakau, Burns wrote a letter to the Japanese authorities at the Passage indicating his desire to give himself up. He dispatched the letter by one of his houseboys. A return message ordered Frank to immediately report to Captain Ito at Sohano. Burns, accompanied by his personal servant, Kati, obtained a small launch from Father Lebel and left Tinputz for the Passage.

According to Kati, Frank was arrested as soon as he set foot on the island. He was escorted to Ito's headquarters where he was interrogated. Later in the day, Kati saw his master taken by armed guards to the jail. The servant was told to make himself scarce as Frank Burns would be remaining in custody on Sohano.

Neither Fred Urban or Father Lebel was able to throw any definite light on the reason for Bums's action. The natives who knew Frank put the blame on Urban. However, Urban insisted that Burns never discussed the matter with him, other than to state that he was writing a note to the Japanese informing them of his intention to surrender. It seemed incredible to me that two men could live together and not discuss such an important decision.

Frank Burns remained a prisoner on Sohano for two or three months and was eventually shipped out, probably to Rabaul. On various occasions my scouts noticed Frank working with a native grass-cutting party—his job being to sweep up the debris.

My own gut feeling was that Urban influenced Burns, either directly or indirectly, and that Frank anticipated a similar parole treatment as was accorded Urban. However, Burns was aware that the Japanese had murdered Percy Good and that Reverend Alley was interned somewhere. There had to be more to this incident—and there was, as I later discovered.

On May 2, I was at my new location, but very much clouded in, when I received a message from Mackie that many enemy warships were anchored in Queen Carola Harbor. His station afforded a view to the west of Buka—but, like mine, it was usually covered with clouds.

By a stroke of luck the sky cleared early the next morning just long enough for me to spot the vessels preparing to put to sea. I immediately sent a message to that effect. Presumably this fleet concentration was associated with the battle of the Coral Sea and the Japanese seizure of Tulagi.

Although VNTG Tulagi was now off the air, Mason and I continued to keep in direct contact with VIG Port Moresby. However, for our own safety, Paul and I seldom communicated with each other. Whenever interisland messages were necessary they were sent through VIG, and we listened for replies at scheduled morning and evening broadcasts.

The small Japanese garrison at Sohano still remained inactive. However, Captain Ito informed the natives that a crack Army unit was due shortly from Rabaul to hunt us down with trained dogs. This report reached me just as I received a message from Lieutenant Commander Feldt to the effect that a special detachment of enemy troops and dogs were operating in New Ireland. But, although this threat remained with us for a long time, it was merely propaganda—as we were never chased by any dogs.

The natives of Buka Island were now staunchly pro-Japanese. All the village chiefs had been summoned to Sohano and were presented with a special armband. Each village also flew the enemy flag. The old chief of Lemankoa Village, however, refused the command to report to Sohano. Whereupon his own countrymen, incited by the Japanese, carried him there by force. The chief was then publicly executed for his disobedience. Other chiefs were subjected to public flogging. This was the enemy's first real act of aggression against local natives—and the lasting effect on these simple people can well be imagined. Allegiance was being exhorted by fear rather than by free will.

The enemy opened a school at the Passage to educate the native children in Japanese lore. Twice weekly the children were brought to the facility, where they learned how to bow toward the Emperor and to all Japanese soldiers. The school was disbanded once the Passage began to get its share of Allied bombing and strafing.

Father McConville related an interesting story about Captain Ito's daily visits to the Tarlena Mission. McConville described the Japanese officer as a would-be ladies' man, and surprisingly tolerant toward the Tarlena people. But, of course, he had a purpose in mind. Captain Ito had designs on the 16-year-old daughter of the half-caste Pitt family that was employed at the mission. When the parents rejected the captain's offer, Ito forced the girl's mother and father to toil for several days building a stone causeway.

In the meantime, suspicions were mounting against Fred Urban. Although Austrian by birth, Urban was a naturalized British subject. In 1914, he had been a German government employee at Kieta when the Australians took formal possession of the town. When I first arrived in Bougainville, I learned that public opinion credited him with pro-Nazi sentiments.

I always suspected that there was a background story to Urban's release versus Alley's internment by the Japanese. I also thought there was more to Frank Burns's surrender than Fred cared to discuss. The latest information I received was that Urban had sought financial assistance from Japanese authorities to enable him to carry on cocoa production at Hakau and that he intended to ship the produce to Sohano.

This report was merely circumstantial, but my attitude was emphatic. Every person on Bougainville had to be either for us or against us—there could be no middle road. The missionaries might be regarded as neutrals, providing they did nothing to prejudice our cause.

I sent a note to Urban, and the tenor of his reply was boldly defiant. He readily admitted having applied to the Japanese for aid, and he blatantly enclosed the original letter he received from Captain Ito.

I conferred with Lieutenant Mackie, and we agreed that something had to be done—but what? We could not afford the encumbrance of having a prisoner on our hands, nor could we sanction consorting with the enemy. It was imperative for our safety that this dangerous complication be resolved. Therefore, a detachment of men under Corporal McLean traveled to Hakau and escorted Urban to Aravia, where Mackie and I conducted a formal interrogation.

Fred Urban agreed, under oath, to answer any and all questions truthfully. His statements were written down in the form of a deposition, which he signed. At the conclusion of the inquiry, I told Urban that he would be removed from Bougainville at the first opportunity—along with the papers concerning the investigation, for their delivery to the proper authorities.

Urban was allowed to return to his plantation under strict conditions that he would do all in his power to prevent further contact between himself and the Japanese. Fred soberly accepted our stipulations, and Lieutenant Mackie sent periodic patrols to Hakau to make sure Urban was abiding by the terms of his release.

About this time, one of the Army scouting parties had discovered an ideal observation post for my coast watching activities. The location was in the mountain range directly behind Soraken—about 2,500 feet above sea level—and commanded a panoramic view of everything north, east, and west of an imaginary line from Soraken Point to Baniu Bay. The site covered all of the Passage and Buka Island. It was about 12 miles from Sohano, and clouds would rarely be a problem.

To reach this location it would be necessary to cut through very difficult bush country into an uninhabited mountain area. I decided to reserve this spot until events justified moving my post—because, no matter how secret our movements, or how inaccessible the site may be, natives would soon be aware of our presence. And, with pro-Japanese people in the vicinity, the information would soon be in enemy hands.

Following negotiations for stores and supplies to be dropped by air, I set out from Aravia with my teleradio team to the Kunua Plantation. The journey west took several days, as we were forced to blaze our own trail through very rugged country rather than taking the beaten paths.

At 9 A.M. of June 7, 1942, in accordance with my instructions, a Hudson bomber from Port Moresby appeared to seaward of the plantation. We lighted two smoke fires on the beach, and the craft banked our way. Barely clearing the tall palms, the pilot made several runs—each time leaving in his wake a package floating down on a white parachute. Unfortunately, the last chute released was caught on the tail of the plane, and it refused to dislodge. The bomber roared over our heads, maneuvering sharply in an effort to shake loose the trailing carton. The plane's gunners attempted to shoot the bundle free, but to no avail. A hand soon waved from the side of the aircraft as it turned and headed into the west—leaving us alone and isolated, standing on the sands of Kunua.

This was our first supply drop—and it was a novel experience. It was also refreshing to again see a plane with our own colors on the side and wings. My gratitude went out to the brave air crew, and to all others responsible for the operation. Among the packages was my first mail from home in many months. The air drop gave a big boost to the morale of the police boys—who, in spite of their avowed loyalty, must have been harboring some misgivings about our future. They now realized that we were not forgotten.

While waiting for the air drop at Kunua, I again met with Father Herbert and Usaia Sotutu. Usaia was still keen on taking an active part in our cause and brought with him a half-caste lad—Anton Jossten. Like Usaia, Anton was very intelligent and spoke English fluently. They had an unusual proposition for me that had immediate appeal. Usaia had a following of educated natives who had been employed as teachers at the Methodist Mission. Usaia and Anton, with the assistance of this group, wanted to establish an espionage network to furnish intelligence regarding Japanese activity around the Buka Passage. The scheme had intriguing possibilities. The teachers were not known to be in any way connected with our coast watching activities. They could move about, within or near enemy lines, without suspicion. I gave Usaia the go-ahead to proceed with his plans. And, although both he and Anton were willing to work voluntarily, I gave them both to understand that I would try and have them enlisted—or put on the payroll in some other capacity.

During the ensuing year, these lads, with ever-increasing risks to themselves, procured a multitude of information that was passed to Station VIG. I do not know for sure, but I believe that their frequent reports—as to the location of enemy fuel dumps, ammunition storage, and aircraft strength around the Passage—must have been a great help to Allied bombers. Two of Usaia's spies were caught by pro-Japanese natives and delivered to Sohano. The informants were sentenced to death, but they managed to escape before the penalty could be carried out.

About the middle of June, Captain Sima relieved Ito as commanding officer at Sohano. Incidentally, I heard that the garrison there was in a bad way. Malaria and dysentery were running rampant and food shortages were reported.

The enemy was beginning to use Soraken as an overnight anchorage for a couple of flying boats that were now patrolling the Bougainville coast. Of more significance, however, was the fact that the Japanese had started reconstruction of the Buka airfield. Hordes of native labor were conscripted for the task. Enemy air traffic also increased, though not to the extent of flight formations. A few isolated landings were noticed on the airstrip, but no planes were stationed there as yet. According to our information, this would come later, as soon as the aerodrome had been enlarged.

By now, however, the Japanese were not the only people with planes in the sky. Single units of our own airforce had dropped a few bombs around the Passage. No damage was done, and enemy propaganda gained a few points in the eyes of the natives—the ploy being that our planes were incapable of causing destruction or even hitting their target. And, of course, bombs that exploded in the water meant just that many more fish for the natives. Our raids in those days were obviously in the nature of a mere gesture, rather than for the purpose of causing material damage—but we were on the eve of doing much better.

I now began to give serious thought to an earlier plan of building a chain of emergency bases to which my party could fall back in event of enemy pressure—which was sure to come eventually. These sites would have to be located in the most inaccessible areas and well off the regular trails.

When the news of my supply drop became known, along with information that Lieutenant Mackie was also expecting a consignment by air, certain members of the European community demanded similar treatment. Mr. Campbell was the self-appointed spokesman for the group. He submitted a list enumerating certain luxury items—their stock of which was either low or depleted. Mr. Campbell demanded that I relay his request to Australian authorities.

These civilians continued to live at their plantation homes unmolested. The Japanese had made no attempts to return to these areas since the one and only visit during March. The Europeans still enjoyed plenty of fresh meat, fish, poultry, vegetables, and other foodstuffs. Fred Urban supplied them with coffee and cocoa. Sea water was condensed for salt. Indigenous cane was rendered to sugar pulp. And corn provided a millet substitute for flour.

Campbell and his cohorts were definitely living better than we were. These were the same people who had repeatedly refused to be evacuated. However, none of them were starving—and had there been the remotest suggestion of hunger and deprivation, my dispatch to headquarters would have been different. As it was, I sent the following message to Lieutenant Commander Feldt:

> Some civilians demand stores be dropped for them. All living on coast. Meat, fish, eggs, milk, and vegetables procurable. No malnutrition. Those demanding had refused to obey December evacuation order and were allowed to stay at own risk. Only if practical deliver enough for all. Recommend flour, sugar, butter, jam, lactogen.

No reply was ever received. I did not expect one, nor did I ever feel justified in following it up.

On July 14, my call sign was changed to that of my daughter's initials—JER. At the same time, Mason was advised to use the first three letters of his sister's surname—STO.

During the month, there was a temporary enemy occupation of Kieta by a small force of 40 men under Captain Osaki. This outfit had just been relieved from garrison duty at Faisi, and they were a sickly lot. Accompanying them was a cultured and clever Jap by the name of Toshiro. During the pre-war years this fellow was well known in Bougainville as a fisherman and trader; however, he was really a Japanese intelligence officer.

Toshiro's assignment at Kieta was that of district manager in the new regime. He addressed an assembly of natives to that effect—telling them that he was about to go to Rabaul and would soon return to exchange their English money for Japanese currency at the rate of two shillings for one yen. However, this occupation had only lasted a few weeks when the enemy suddenly packed up their gear and withdrew.

Bishop Wade made his first contact with the Japanese during their short stay at Kieta. He was not treated harshly and was placed on parole with instructions not to leave town. But when the Japs abandoned the city, Wade considered himself no longer bound by his parole and he escaped to northern Bougainville.

By the end of July, several enemy antiaircraft gun positions had been set up at Sohano, and coastal artillery was emplaced at strategic locations around the Passage. Also, large contingents of native labor had finished lengthening and improving the Buka airstrip.

Lieutenant Mackie and I discussed possible sneak attacks on these Japanese installations. However, we did not wish to jeopardize our personnel unless the target merited taking casualties. Ours was an intelligence job only, and we could not risk any enemy attention that might put us off the air.

On August 3, my air drop request for the Army was approved. An ideal site had been found and cleared in the middle of the old coffee plantation at Rugen—inland from Raua Bay. One of our aircraft, on reconnaissance patrol, inspected and approved the location. The drop was scheduled for late night, and I moved my teleradio to the spot for the occasion. Our instructions were to set a fire-stack [woodpile] at each corner of the clearing—ready to light when the plane was heard.

Shortly after midnight, the steady drone of a Catalina flying boat filtered through the night air—becoming louder as it approached the plantation. The fires were lit, and we watched silently as the aircraft circled to a lower altitude. Illuminated by the glow of flames, the Catalina stood out in bold relief against the dark background of sky. My entire body quivered with excitement as the pilot made his first of several dead-center runs—no more than a hundred feet above the field.

Mackie's men were now enjoying the same thrill that I had experienced at Kunua—the fires lighting up our colors under the wing as the plane roared overhead. Each run revealed a white parachute unfolding from one side gun blister, while several less elegant bundles tumbled down from the opposite gun port. After his last drop, the pilot gave us a final run for the road, and his signal gun flashed out "Good luck" as he disappeared into the blackness.

We knew it was difficult and dangerous to supply such a small outpost as ours, and therefore we fully appreciated the five chutes and 31 parcels that we received. One package far outweighed the others. It was a bag of mail for the lads—their first since last Christmas. By dawn the native helpers had gathered up the shipment and were ready for their arduous trek up the Ramasan Valley to Matahai, while I returned to my base behind Aravia.

I had previously notified Lieutenant Commander Feldt about the forward observation site that Mackie's scouts had located for me in the mountains behind Soraken—and that I was prepared to move to the area upon his signal.

On August 5, 1942, I received urgent instructions to proceed immediately to the Soraken position and to commence reporting all enemy sightings and any activity pertaining to the Buka airfield. Mason, at his forward base overlooking Buin, received similar orders—with special emphasis on Japanese ship movements in the Bougainville Straits. The messages contained no other information, but it was enough to indicate that a major military operation was about to take place somewhere in the Solomons.

Within two days, my new teleradio station was set up and working. Our coast watching activities were now about to begin in earnest.

CHAPTER 4

Setting Up the Southern Bougainville Coast Watching Station

MARCH 6–AUGUST 7, 1942

Paul Mason

M y coast station watching at Inus, overlooking Kieta Harbor, became a headquarters and a clearinghouse of information. At times my resources were somewhat strained in extending hospitality. On one occasion, I had 13 people living at the post all holding conferences from which I remained aloof. I listened to their stories of trials and tribulations and to their plans, but I felt that there was too much irrelevant discussion. Besides, I was kept continually busy feeding them and sending not only their signals but mine as well.

Four AIF personnel had been assigned to Kieta—Warner, McGarrell, White, and Johnston. And four other soldiers—Wigley, Otton, Ross, and Swanson—were sent down to Buin.

Unfortunately my native police spotters had been placed under Warner's command, and, therefore, I received my sighting reports secondhand. On one occasion, the boys told Warner that a Japanese warship had entered Kieta Harbor during the night, but I did not receive the message until 9 the following morning.

I complained to Lieutenant Commander Feldt and was given permission to disassociate myself from the Army authority and to find another location. I was unarmed and would now

be without a police boy, but I selected a safe spot north of
Kieta. I knew that in case of an enemy invasion the town was
actually a death trap—but I could not convince the soldiers of
the danger. The AIF went merrily on their way—playing the
game of administration and imprisoning natives implicated in
the January lootings. I tried to convince the Army lads that
they were living in a fool's paradise—and forming an organization that was certain to collapse upon the arrival of the enemy.

At Lieutenant Mackie's direction, the soldiers had mobi-
lized all available police to guard the many natives that had
been arrested. Consequently, I was unable to find any boys to
man my coast watching post. It seemed that I was the only person in Kieta who took coast watching seriously.

Toward the end of March, I was notified that the Japanese
had occupied the Buka Passage, they had shelled and landed
on Faisi in the Shortlands, and their warships had been sighted
off Buin. On the 31st, Station VNTG sent a message that four
cruisers and a transport were proceeding from the Passage and
down the Bougainville coast.

I feared a Japanese raid on Kieta and sent a letter by runner
to the AIF lads who were living it up in town. These guys, with
their radio and other luxuries scrounged from deserted homes,
had been taking life too easy. My note warned them that I
expected the enemy force to arrive the next morning. I also
notified the missionaries. Bishop Wade had already instructed
his people to try and avoid meeting the Japs—if it could be
done without leaving their parishes.

I posted a few willing native spotters at vantage points above
Kieta, but the enemy ships were not sighted until daylight. They
proved to be four destroyers and a supply vessel. Two of the
destroyers remained outside the harbor, while the other ships
landed troops on either side of the peninsula. Six float planes
flew air cover for the operation.

Just before midday, the raiding force returned to their ships
and continued south. One Japanese aircraft remained behind
for quite some time, apparently searching the hills for me.

After notifying VIG and VNTG about the raid, I hurried down to Kieta. On the way, I met up with Warner and McGarrell. They were also returning to town after visiting with Tom Ebery at Toimonapu. While we were discussing the situation, Johnston and White showed up—covered with mud. They had sat up talking practically all night at the Police Master's quarters, and toward morning, they had decided to hike up the hill toward the native police post to check if the watch was alert. During the climb they heard Japanese voices. A sudden flare illuminated the enemy troops, but the AIF soldiers were kept in the shadows.

Johnston and White raced down the hill to their quarters and tried to awaken the native houseboys, who, in native fashion, had locked themselves in. The AIF lads burst down the door, grabbed their packs, and headed to the harbor area. However, a Japanese patrol was spotted on the road below, and the two soldiers were forced to take cover in a creek bed. Later in the morning, they climbed to a cliff overlooking the bay to see if the enemy ships had left.

Wong You had taken to the hills the night before. When he returned, he discovered his store torn apart and plundered.

When the Japanese force landed at Kieta, five missionaries were living at the mission—Fathers Tonjes and Seiller and Brothers Severius, Jules, and Henry. Jules cleared out upon hearing that the enemy had arrived, but the others remained and greeted the Japanese.

Brother Henry, who I think is a bit simple and everybody's fool, began blabbering his head off while he was being interrogated. From what I was able to find out, he revealed the location of the AIF at Buin, and he even disclosed information about my coast watching activities. Henry also talked about Kroening, the white flag incident, and Merrylees's frantic evacuation.

The enemy employed a former Japanese resident of Kieta, named Toshiro, as their interpreter. Toshiro had been on friendly terms with most Europeans on Bougainville, including

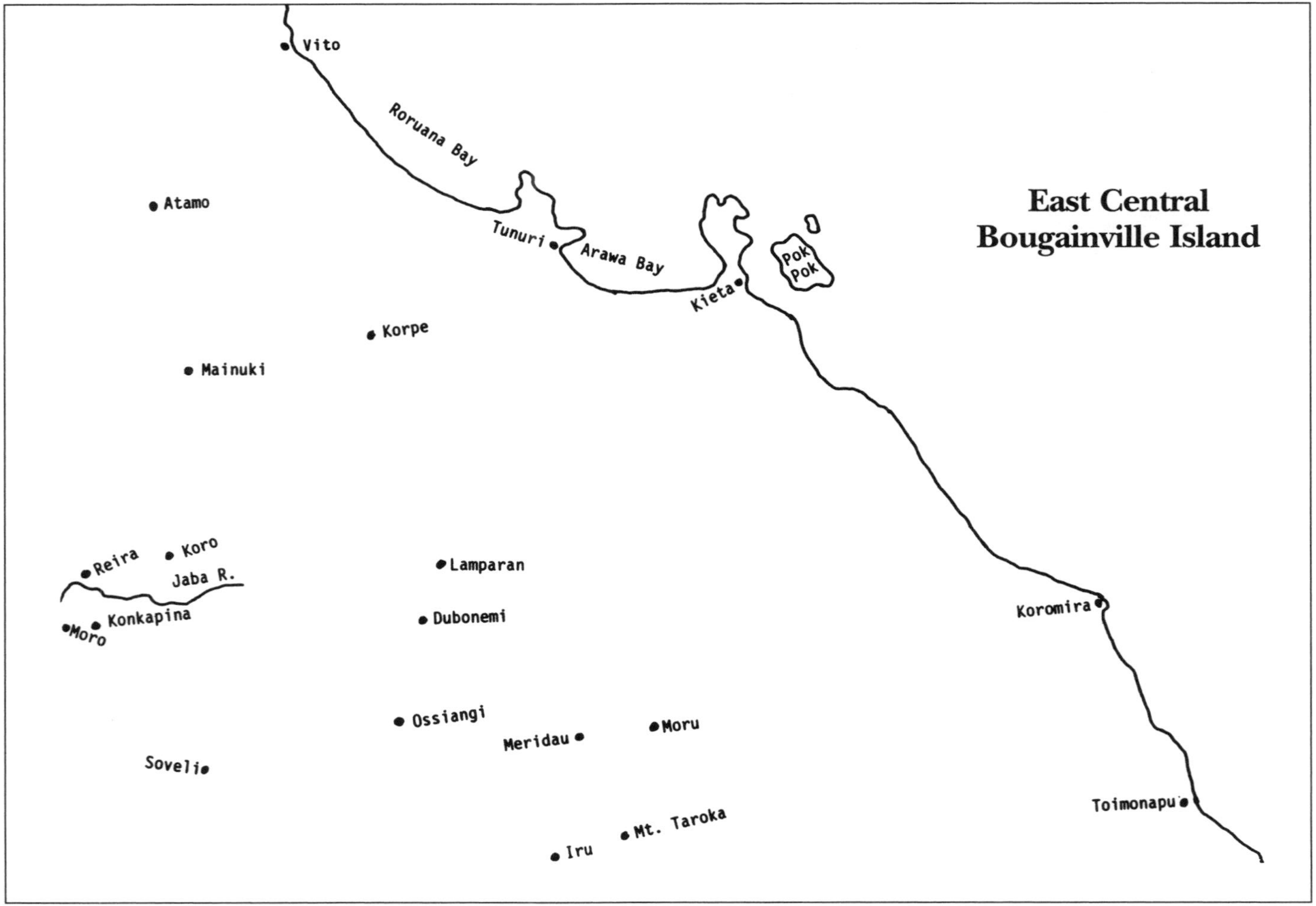
East Central
Bougainville Island
Vito
Roruana Bay
Tunuri
Arawa Bay
Kieta
Pok Pok
Atamo
Korpe
Mainuki
Reira
Koro
Jaba R.
Lamparan
Konkapina
Moro
Dubonemi
Koromira
Ossiangi
Meridau
Moru
Soveli
Toimonapu
Mt. Taroka
Iru

the missionaries. In pre-war days, I had learned to know him quite well—and I formed the opinion that he was very crafty. After Pearl Harbor, Australian authorities interned Toshiro at Rabaul, but he escaped and fled to Truk.

During their rampage at Kieta, the Japanese looted the AIF supplies. Therefore, Warner and his men decided to abandon the town and head for the government storage dump at Mainuki. They tried to convince me to go with them, but I pointed out that my coast watching job was too important for the war effort. We parted company and were not destined to meet again for 12 months.

I signaled Wigley at Buin that his location had been betrayed to the enemy. However, he and his detachment refused to leave their comfortable quarters at Kangu House. About the middle of April a Japanese patrol chased them out. Wigley's party lost everything—including their teleradio.

On Easter Sunday, April 5, I went down to the Kieta Mission and learned that Father Tonjes and Brother Henry were spreading Japanese propaganda to the effect that the Nipponese had occupied the island and the war in Bougainville was over. These fictitious rumors were beginning to have a detrimental effect on the population. One native remarked that Father Tonjes had told him to kill me. However, after living many years in this area, I knew the people very well and took no notice of this kind of chatter. In fact, later on, the natives betrayed the missionaries first.

Before the enemy departed from Kieta, Toshiro had left a letter for Wong You—instructing him to go to Faisi and work for the Japanese. The missionaries attempted to convince the Chinaman to obey the order: "After all, you must think first of your wife and children and the other Chinese on the island." Wong was panic-stricken and appealed to me for advice. I hustled down to the mission and tackled Brother Henry. I also wrote a strong letter to Bishop Wade. The bishop put a quick stop to the harassment, and Wong You was no longer pestered. Father Tonjes was later removed to a parish well away from Kieta.

By this time, I had acquired two houseboys and was notified by Lieutenant Commander Feldt of my appointment as a petty officer in the Navy.

But rumors continued to persist. I was secretly informed that a group of natives intended to loot a government supply facility at Daratui. The village was inland, due west of Kieta, and I headed there immediately. The dump was guarded by one police boy who considered me a civilian because I was not wearing a uniform and was unarmed.

Much to my surprise, Father Tonjes showed up, clicking his heels (he had been a German soldier at one time). He found me in low spirits, wandering about in the midst of a jumble of unsorted cargo. I questioned him about the rumor of the natives intending to raid the stores. Tonjes claimed that he tried to explain to the people that the supplies did not belong to them—but to whatever government was in charge of the island. However, he did admit telling the villagers that Bougainville was under Japanese control. He also told me that when the natives asked if they should kill me, he discouraged the idea. I was determined not to be intimidated by the priest and informed him that it was not the way I heard the story.

Tonjes tried to shrug off the rumor by remarking that this was typical of the way natives twisted a man's words. He advised me not to trust the villagers, saying they would sell me for a stick of tobacco. Tonjes seemed to be sympathetic toward me, but he regarded my position as hopeless and wanted me to face the facts. He definitely was not pro-Japanese. However, he did not conceal his anti-English feelings, either.

To some extent, religious differences among the villagers decided the policy of the people. On the whole, Japanese propaganda was more successful with the Catholic natives because of the priest's official policy of neutrality in the war. The Seventh-Day Adventist and Methodist missions were clearly anti-Japanese, but most of their clergy had already left the island.

I had no sooner returned to my coast watching station when a runner delivered a note from Wigley—asking me to prepare hot tea and coffee for some hungry troops. Within the hour, four tired and bedraggled AIF soldiers from Buin stumbled into camp. In no time at all, my houseboys whipped up plenty of hot food and drink while Wigley related their narrow escape from the enemy.

On Easter Sunday morning, the AIF lads were shaving and getting dressed before breakfast when they suddenly heard the engine noises of boats. Their first glance seaward revealed Japanese troops scrambling ashore from barges. An armed schooner covered the assault.

Wigley and his men slammed the wireless set to the floor, smashing it to bits, and raced up the hill behind the house. The Australians could hear the Jap soldiers shouting and screaming as they charged into the dwelling.

From a vantage point on the side of the hill, Ross asked permission to open up on the Nips with his tommy gun, But Wigley, realizing his men were greatly outnumbered, ordered the AIF boys to withdraw. However, once across the hill, they lost their way in the swamps on the other side. The soldiers jettisoned most of their gear in order to travel faster and, about noon, they reached Chong You's store at Turiboiru, where the Chinaman fixed a quick meal for the lads.

The AIF men hacked their way inland, through 25 miles of thick jungle growth, until they reached the west coast. They tried to convince a small group of native fishermen to take them by canoe to the Treasury Islands. But the soldiers had no conception of the distance involved. They would never have made the crossing safely.

The natives did, however, tell Wigley that I had fled to the storage depot at Daratui and was probably now back at my base camp. The Army boys, expecting to find good things on my table, cut across country to join me. I had been ill for several days, but after the AIF lads arrived, my health improved rapidly. And soon I was able to eat nearly as well as the soldiers—and they were large eaters. Fortunately, the local natives supplied us with plenty of provisions, and my houseboys cooked bigger and bigger meals until the food had to be brought to the table in deep washbowls—filled to the brim.

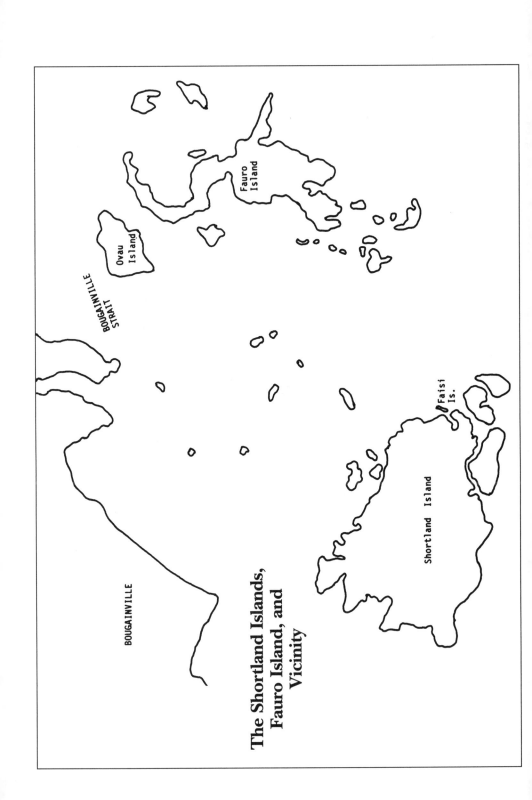

**The Shortland Islands,
Fauro Island, and
Vicinity**

BOUGAINVILLE

BOUGAINVILLE
STRAIT

Ovau
Island

Fauro
Island

Shortland Island

Faisi
Is.

Early in April, I had received permission from Lieutenant Commander Feldt to establish a coast watching post near Buin. I had hesitated because I was unarmed and without a police boy. However, with the arrival of the soldiers, I was now ready to set off on the journey. I invited Wigley and Otton to accompany me.

Wigley and I headed south by road, while Otton, because of a bad leg, traveled by canoe. When we reached Toimonapu, I climbed into the hills to see Tom Ebery—who was in hiding and very sick. Bishop Wade was with him. Wade was very concerned with the situation on Bougainville. He had the responsibility of keeping his mission going with a staff of mixed nationalities, while his own country was at war with Japan. He was especially anxious about the future safety of the Sisters at the mission.

After leaving Toimonapu, we moved inland, gradually ascending the mountains to the village of Nantokina on the crest of a 2,000-foot range. On April 30, my birthday, I led my men across the Luluai Valley, then over the pass joining the Crown Prince and Deuro Mountain ranges, to the village of Omgu.

On the afternoon of May 1, we arrived at Kikibatsiago and made camp. During the night, our sleep was continually interrupted by the sound of aircraft engines roaring overhead and the noise of explosions in the distance. The following morning, I bicycled down to the beach at Kahili to investigate. I learned from the natives that Japanese ships had been attacked by planes northwest of Shortland Island. This was probably one of the phases of the Coral Sea engagement.

Wigley and I spent the next couple of days hunting for a suitable observation site in the vicinity of Mituai. I finally selected a spot on Malabita Hill. From this position, I was able to view the entire Buin-Tonolei area.

I set up my teleradio station at Laguai—about nine miles northwest of Buin. In establishing a coast watching base, it was my practice to select a location from which all enemy activity— naval, military, and air—could be seen, and then to choose a spot for the transmitter as far removed as practicable from the observation post. This was a useful safety measure, especially when the teleradio site itself was suitable for the sighting of aircraft. At times, it was necessary to forego precautionary measures and to move the transmitter close to the lookout position so that Japanese planes could be reported without delay. Lieutenant Commander Feldt changed my call signal to STO.

I procured two bicycles, which gave us quick mobility along the roads and paths in the area. During periods when there were no Japs ashore at Buin, I placed native observers on Kangu Hill—which was practically on the coast. But when enemy troops landed, the watchers withdrew to Malabita Hill.

I was beginning to run short of stores, and I arranged with Feldt for a supply drop even though I had not yet decided on a safe location for the operation. A few days later, however, I received a signal that provisions had been dropped by air at Mamarega, about 70 miles west of my location.

I left Wigley and Otton in charge—instructing them to report anything unusual to Station VIG—and, taking a bicycle, I headed for the drop zone. While traveling over a rough section of road, I had a flat, so I walked the bike ten miles to Piano, where I was able to locate a new tube and tire.

When I finally reached Mamarega, I searched for two days, but I was unable to find the supplies. Disgusted at this waste of valuable time, I returned to the coast watching station and notified Lieutenant Commander Feldt that the stores were not at the specified location. I was informed that there was a mixup in communications and the drop had been made at Mutapina Point on Empress Augusta Bay.

While I was away, Wigley and Otton had noticed a great deal of Japanese shipping activity off the Buin coast. Battleships were also observed, but, due to a transmitter breakdown, Wigley was unable to signal the departure of the ships.

Frustrated by the earlier attempt to receive supplies, I again contacted Feldt and arranged for stores to be dropped by a Catalina at Tabararoi Village on the Molika River. The drop took place about midnight on June 2. Unfortunately, it took us three weeks to recover all the chutes—most of the dumps had splashed into the river.

During the middle of June, I heard that certain people from the village of Languai had been in contact with the Japanese. Our activities were in jeopardy. The natives needed to be taught a lesson. We grabbed the village *tul-tul* (interpreter and assistant to the *luluai*, or chief), hauled him before the assembled villagers, and carefully explained that the *tul-tul* was going to receive the punishment for the entire village. I gave the *tul-tul* ten pats on his backside, and we had no more trouble from this group of natives from then on.

About this time, I was instructed by Station VIG to maintain radio silence, except for reporting major enemy movements—or matters relating to our own safety. As coast watchers, we understood our role in this war was to be that of observers. We were not intended to conduct offensive operations against the enemy.

However, it seemed that every single day brought with it more problems. A police boy by the name of Buia related stories of native unrest in the Siwai region, which adjoined the Buin District. I sent Otton and Wigley to find out the reason for the trouble. It all boiled down to the fact that there was no governing official in the district.

I immediately appointed Wigley and Otton as District Officers of Siwai, and native morale rapidly improved. The two soldiers enjoyed their newfound authority and had a great deal of fun arbitrating cases in the native courts. In fact, they became quite proud of their bench work.

In settling native disputes, many humorous situations arose. We also learned that our activities remained secret as long as the people brought their arguments to us for settlement. Even the losing party recognized our authority. In localities where the natives did not bring their cases to us, it meant that they endorsed the enemy. In order to keep the natives cognizant of our jurisdiction, we issued the following propa-

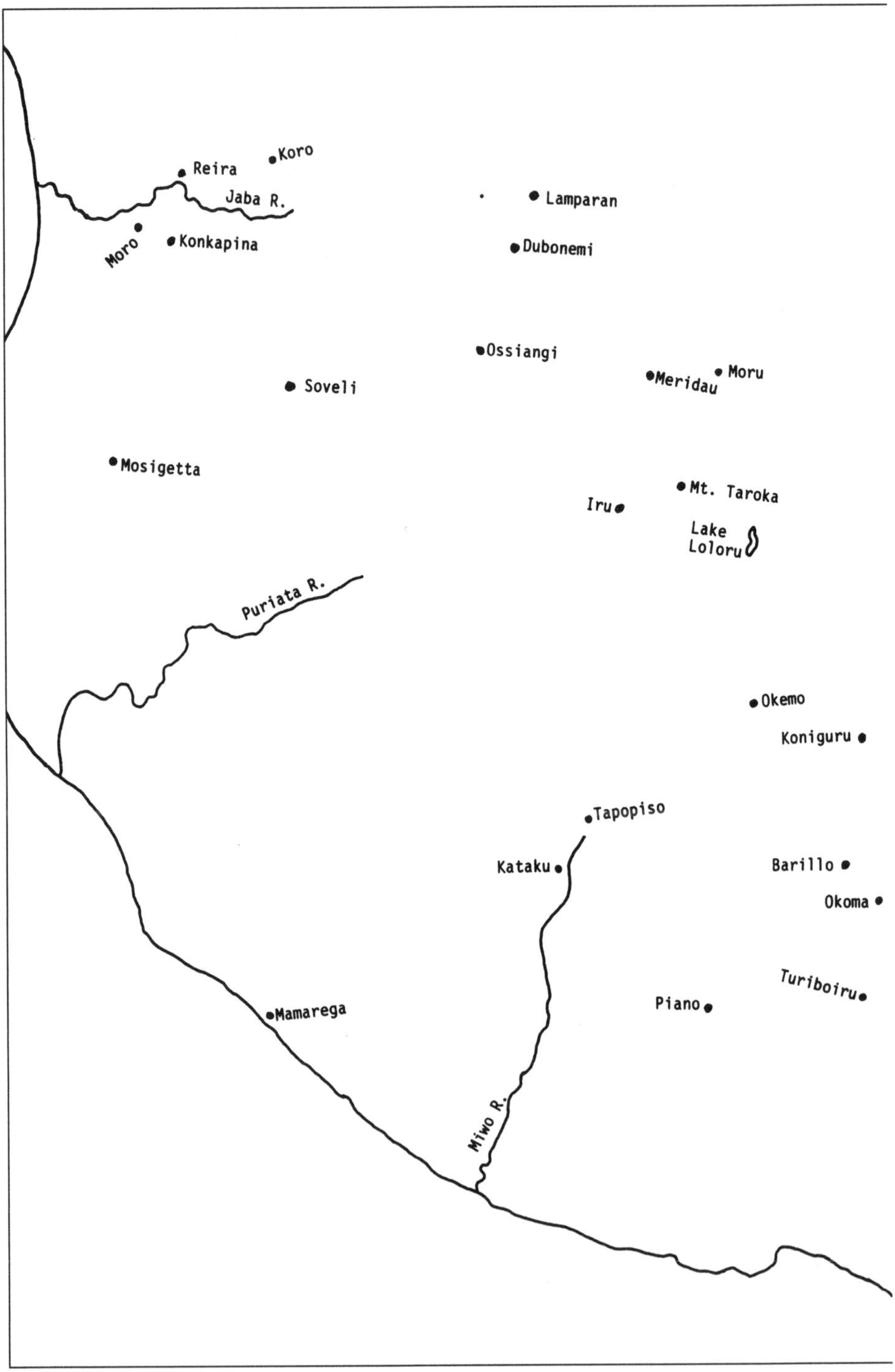

Koro
Reira
Jaba R.
Lamparan
Moro
Konkapina
Dubonemi
Ossiangi
Moru
Meridau
Soveli
Mosigetta
Mt. Taroka
Iru
Lake
Loloru
Puriata R.
Okemo
Koniguru
Tapopiso
Kataku
Barillo
Okoma
Turiboiru
Piano
Mamarega
Miwo R.

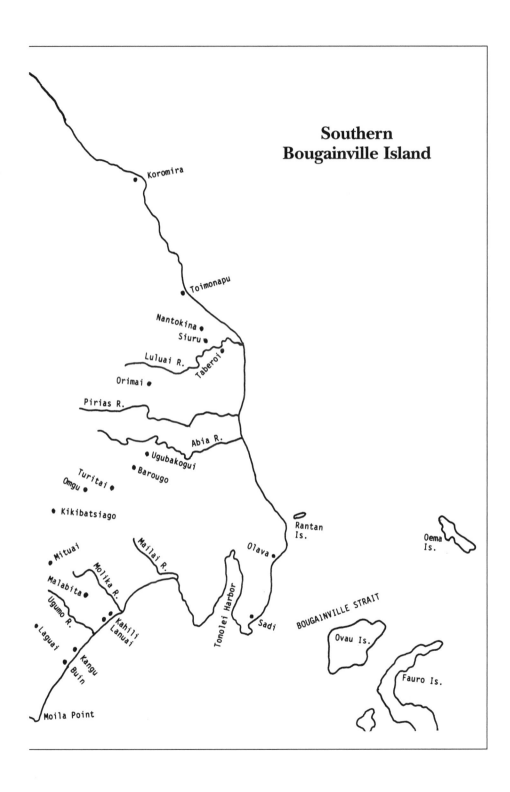

**Southern
Bougainville Island**

Koromira

Toimonapu

Nantokina
Siuru

Luluai R.
Taberoi

Orimai

Pirias R.

Abia R.

Ugubakogui

Turitai
Omgu • Barougo

Kikibatsiago

Rantan
Is.

Oema
Is.

Mituai

Mailai R.

Olava

Molika R.

Malabita

Ugumo R.

Kahili
Lanuai

Tonolei Harbor

Sadi

BOUGAINVILLE STRAIT

Laguai

Kangu
Buin

Ovau Is.

Fauro Is.

Moila Point

ganda notice: "We are here to let the U.S. forces know where the Japanese are located, and where the friendly natives are situated. Unless we are allowed to remain, the U.S. forces will not know friend from foe." The majority of the people in the Buin District accepted this statement as the explanation for our presence and remained friendly—even when they were working for the Japanese.

During July, I received information that an enemy detachment had landed at Kieta, so I sent a runner to scout the town. He returned and reported that the local natives had gone over to the Japs. The district tul-tul was also trying to have the Japs come south and hunt us down. Not taking any chances, I removed our operation to Okemo.

I signaled Port Moresby of the situation and was censured for sending this message. I was told to keep wireless silence and move ten miles from Okemo. I used my own discretion and set up my teleradio at Tambarina, 3,000 feet above sea level, which was the nearest village to Lake Loloru.

We maintained complete radio silence in the hills for ten days, during which time I made several trips to the lake—the object being to determine if it was suitable for a permanent safe base. Loloru is a crater lake at an altitude of 6,000 feet and is hemmed in by hills. No food is grown at this height, and wood for construction and fire is scarce. We made a raft from bamboo poles and used fishing line to lash it together. The weather was cold and wet, but these visits to the lake proved valuable. If supplies could be packed so that they floated, an air drop on the lake would permit us to rescue the cartons and live safely ashore.

By the end of July 1942, there had still been no permanent enemy occupation of Buin—but only weekly visits for scouting purposes and foraging.

On August 4, I requested a supply drop at Kataku on the Miwo River and sent Otton with a party to retrieve the bundles. However, this time the Catalina pilot unloaded the stores into the Puriata swamp—about 20 miles west of Kataku. After a long search, we recovered only one parachute.

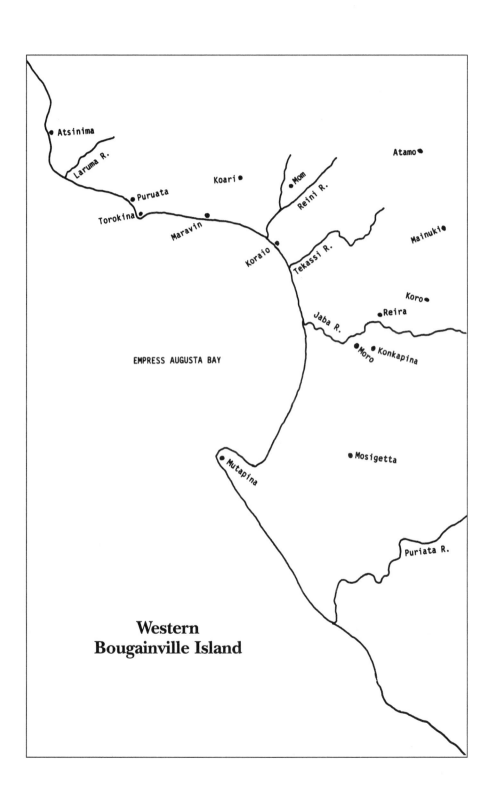

Atsinima

Laruma R.

Atamo

Koari

Mom

Reini R.

Puruata

Torokina

Maravin

Mainuki

Koraio

Tekassi R.

Koro

Jaba R.

Reira

Moro Konkapina

EMPRESS AUGUSTA BAY

Mosigetta

Mutapina

Puriata R.

Western
Bougainville Island

The very next day, I received a signal from VIG to set up shop at our old location at Malabita Hill—and to report all Japanese ship and aircraft movements heading southeast. I suspected that an Allied attack in the Solomons was only hours away.

CHAPTER 5

Air Battles at Guadalcanal

AUGUST 8, 1942–JANUARY 1, 1943

Jack Read

My first intimation of the long-awaited Allied move against the Japanese came on the morning of August 8, 1942. I had just concluded my daily scheduled report to Station VIG and received orders to proceed immediately to Porapora—my new forward observation post behind Soraken. Before dismantling the teleradio, however, I decided to make a quick check of the frequencies for any interesting transmissions. I suddenly picked up a broadcast that made me forget for a moment my departure for Porapora.

I found myself listening to what was obviously the control tower of an aircraft carrier and its planes out on various assignments. The two-way conversations—and the mention of familiar place names around Tulagi—indicated that the island was already in U.S. hands.

While I was sitting mesmerized, absorbing all the details and interpreting them to my boys, Sergeant Yauwika pricked up his ears. Within a few seconds we all heard it—coming from the northwest: the dull, ever-increasing sound of a host of planes approaching our location. Some of the lads climbed to the tree tops as our view was obscured from that direction.

In a matter of moments, the largest aircraft formation I had ever seen raced across a break in the jungle. With their propeller blades glistening in the sun, 27 Japanese dive-bombers roared across the sky in the direction of Tulagi. Minutes later, another squadron of 18 aircraft of the same type passed only a few hundred feet over our heads.

I flashed an immediate message to VIG Port Moresby. It was relayed to Station VIT Townsville, Australia—and was in the hands of Tulagi Control within ten minutes.

Due to the urgency of a report of this kind, the time factor was all important. Consequently, I transmitted in plain language to avoid the time required for coding and decoding. The risk of enemy interception of my signal, and the location of its source, was one that had to be taken. The results were worth it.

I continued to sit by the teleradio receiver. The minutes slowly ticked off my watch. Only jungle noises interrupted the quiet suspense. Suddenly the carrier, alerted of a possible attack, began recalling its aircraft, one by one, to refuel—then each plane quickly dispatched to a high altitude, ready and waiting for the approaching Japanese.

A few minutes after 11 A.M., Tulagi Control detected the large formation of enemy aircraft approaching the U.S. transport area. A voice from the carrier's tower calmly advised its fighter planes that the ships were about to be attacked by at least 40 bombers and that he would quit transmitting during the air battle.

The radio operator's intention to cut off his broadcasting was probably honest in that respect. Nevertheless, he flashed back on the air a few seconds later with a spontaneous and dramatic description of the conflict occurring hundreds of feet in the sky: "Boy! We're shooting 'em down like flies! What a sight! I can see one . . . two . . . three . . . eight of 'em splashing into the sea!" The rapid, staccato ring of his words, and their meaning, imbued me—although 500 miles away—with the same tense excitement with which they were rapped out.

Several minutes passed by before the voice came back on the air. Once again, calm and soberly, the radio operator announced that the attack had been made at a low altitude and at least 12 enemy planes had been shot down—with little damage done to the transport area. I felt proud that my coast watching crew had played some part, however minor, in the successful repulse of the Japanese assault.

The reporting of these enemy flights soon became routine, but I shall never forget the thrill and euphoria of that first morning.

On August 12, Station JER was well established at Porapora. Lieutenant Mackie assigned Signalman Sly to me on a permanent basis. By this time, Sly was thoroughly capable of running the station in my absence, and he was also dependable to have around in case of trouble.

From every angle, I could not wish for a better coast watching site than Porapora. A panoramic view revealed the clustered palms of Soraken 2,500 feet below—with the western sea beyond—and swept over Matchin Bay, with its guardian fringe of atolls that stretched northward along the west coast of Buka to Queen Carola Harbor. We were able to observe all of Buka Island—the airfield and the Passage—and from Bonis, down the east coast of Bougainville, as far south as Baniu Bay. Besides all these advantages, Porapora offered a maximum of security against any surprise venture of the enemy.

Shortly after the American landing on Guadalcanal, Lieutenant Commander Hugh Mackenzie, Royal Australian Navy, was assigned as Deputy Supervising Intelligence Officer, and Station KEN began operating from a base near Henderson Field.

Although Mackenzie and his staff were in charge of the various coast watching posts in the islands, Bougainville remained under direct control of Lieutenant Commander Feldt at Townsville. My job was to keep both officers informed through VIG and KEN—the latter being particularly interested in enemy air raids.

My reports of shipping in and around Buka Passage, though valuable to a degree, never attained the importance of Mason's description of Japanese ship movements in the Buin area.

Warnings of impending enemy air attacks on Guadalcanal and Tulagi, giving the Allies two hours advance notice, were the main objectives of our base at Porapora.

Air strikes against Allied positions in the Solomons were staged from the Japanese stronghold at Rabaul. Large formations of aircraft were employed. And, invariably, their southeasterly course to the American beachhead took them directly over Porapora. Often, while the enemy planes were still within sight and sound, our curt, plain-language signal—advising the exact fighter and bomber strength—was in Mackenzie's hands.

The average flight time from Porapora to Guadalcanal was usually two and a quarter hours. This lengthy warning enabled the various Allied commands to prepare accordingly. Shipping could be disbursed from highly vulnerable concentrated areas to widely scattered positions of maximum safety. And fighter aircraft had time to be fueled, armed, and dispatched to high altitudes—ready to pounce on the attacking force. In addition, naval warships were able to form a defensive antiaircraft perimeter around the beachhead. The element of surprise—the best weapon in any assault—was taken away from the Japanese. That meant that coast watching alone was responsible for the success of the air war.

Each evening, during his scheduled broadcast, Mackenzie would notify the coast watching stations—advising them of the score—whenever there had been a strike against Guadalcanal. This tally was usually about 20 to one in our favor. On a few occasions, the enemy bombers lost their complete fighter escort.

Practically every day, we would watch the awe-inspiring, streamlined formations of Japanese planes heading southward over our position. Then, five or six hours later, whatever was left of the attacking force straggled home in small groups for an hour or more. Aircraft, unable to make Rabaul, found a safe haven at the Buka airfield—but many of them crash-landed.

There were other coast watchers south of Bougainville who also contributed their share toward warning Guadalcanal of impending raids. I refer to Nick Waddell on Choiseul, Henry Josselyn on Vella Lavella, and Donald Kennedy on New Georgia.

My own location at Porapora was geographically at the head of the line, enabling me to warn Station KEN 30 minutes earlier than Mason at Buin and an hour or more ahead of the other stations.

Frequently, my report was the only message to give the exact Japanese bomber and escort strength—by reason of the fact that the enemy formations flew over Porapora at a low altitude and then commenced to climb to a greater height. Observers farther south were invariably handicapped by the increased altitude and attendant cloud banks. Hence, quite a number of their reports were based on sound rather than on actually sighting the aircraft. However, if this signal happened to be the first warning received by KEN, it was every bit as valuable as direct observation.

Occasionally, enemy formations from the northwest did not pass over Bougainville until they reached the southwest coast. But I believe that Mason was able to pick up whatever I missed in that respect.

During the early part of the Solomon Islands offensive, the Japanese hurled daily massive air strikes from Rabaul in an effort to frustrate the American invasion of Tulagi and Guadalcanal. But these constant attacks were soon slowed, due to the timely warnings emanating from Bougainville. The success of our organization is evident from the appreciative signal I received from Mason on August 18: "Commander Task Forces Tulagi and Guadalcanal has expressed appreciation of air attack warnings given by you."

In August and September, enemy activity around the Buka Passage increased greatly. The Japanese had suffered an unexpected setback in the Solomons. Therefore, they were forced to consolidate bases that otherwise would have been accorded only a nominal detachment of troops. The garrison at Sohano was reinforced with several hundred men, and additional ground crews had been sent to the airstrip.

The Buka field was developing into the main feature of the Passage. The Japanese had enlarged the strip—and, although

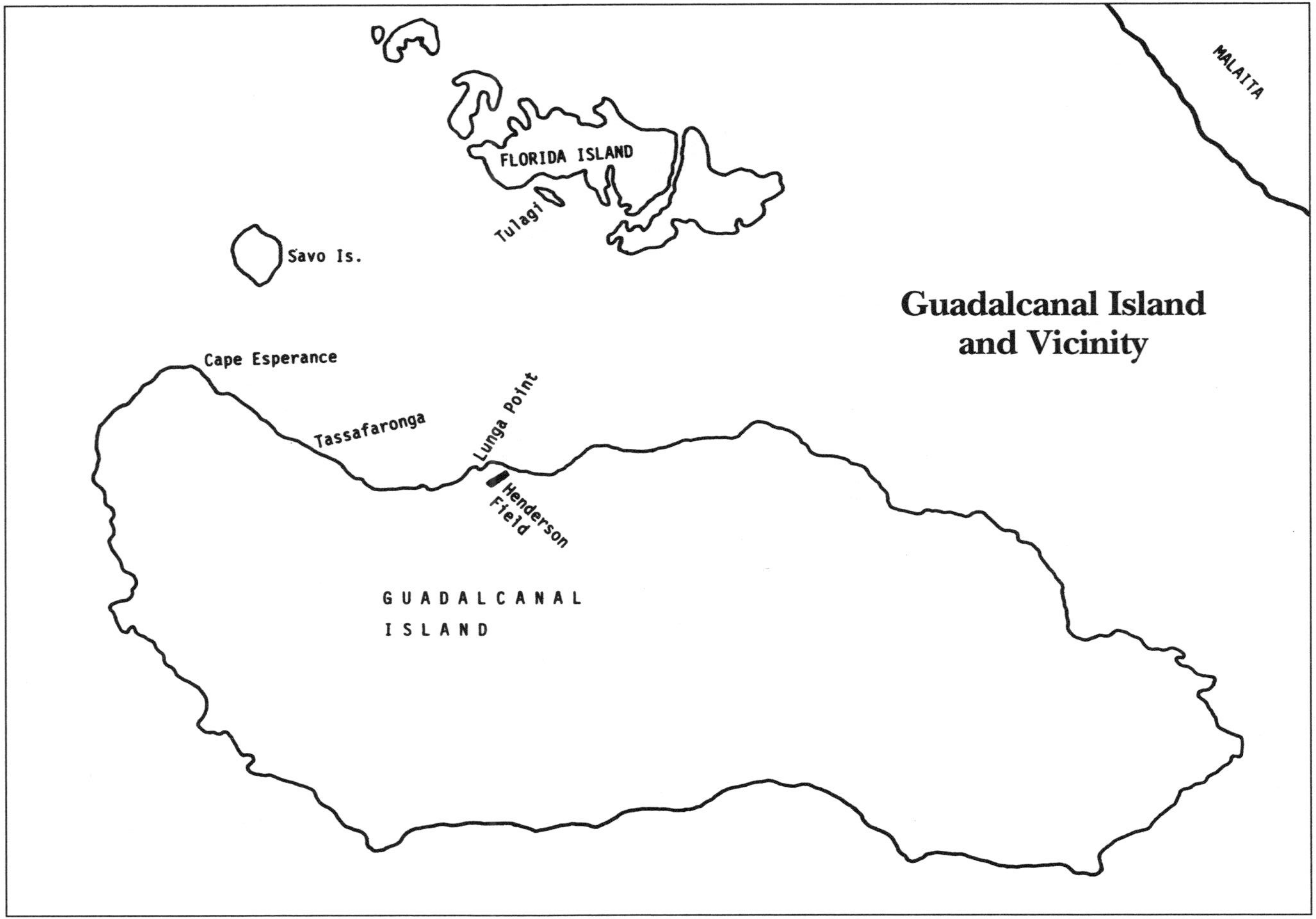
Guadalcanal Island
and Vicinity
MALAITA
FLORIDA ISLAND
Tulagi
Savo Is.
Cape Esperance
Tassafaronga
Lunga Point
Henderson
Field
GUADALCANAL
ISLAND

few bombers occasionally landed, the airfield was used mainly as a fighter base.

The 700-mile hop from Rabaul to the southern Solomons, and return, did not permit the Zeros to stay more than a few minutes over the target area. Consequently, there was a growing tendency for enemy aircraft formations to pick up their fighter escorts from Buka—200 miles closer to Guadalcanal.

From our grandstand location at Porapora, it was rather an impressive sight to watch several squadrons of Japanese heavy bombers come out of the northwest in perfect order. They circled lazily over Buka, while Zeros took off in pairs from the airfield below. As soon as the fighters trimmed into the formation, the fleet of from 40 to 60 planes would head south—many of them never to return.

The Buka airstrip also began to suffer from Allied night raids. On several occasions, the damage inflicted was particularly heavy. Usaia Sotutu and his team of scouts reported severe casualties in personnel and many planes destroyed on the ground.

One of the heaviest attacks on the Passage was carried out on the night of September 2, 1942. Under cover of darkness, three Japanese warships, believed to be a light cruiser and two destroyers, entered the strait. When our bombers came over, these ships opened fire. A stick of bombs straddled one of the vessels, silencing its antiaircraft guns. The following dawn revealed only two of the ships at anchor. Later in the day, an official communiqué broadcast over the air stated that a destroyer had been bombed with unknown results. Either the vessel sank immediately or else it slipped out of the Passage before daybreak.

One of the many precautions we had to take to throw the enemy off our scent was the change of call signs. On September 11, my signal was switched to BTU, and Mason's became LQK.

By late September, we were again becoming short of supplies. And two air drops by Catalinas were scheduled at the

Rugen Plantation—one for the night of September 23 and the other for October 1. Lieutenant Mackie took charge of the operation while I remained at Porapora.

Weather conditions were not the best on the first night—heavy clouds obscured the moon—and the pilot was forced to make the drop from too high an altitude. As a result, several of the chutes drifted, falling into the jungle quite a distance from the clearing. The natives of Tetsiko, a small village adjoining Rugen, had been employed as workers for the operation. Their job was to gather the stores and transport them up the Ramasan Valley to the AIF base at Matahai. After a lengthy search, the natives alleged that they were unable to find the chutes, which had fallen wide of the mark. Mackie had no option but to give up all hope of recovering the supplies. Shortly afterward, however, we were informed that the Tetsiko people had located the parachutes and were intending to recover the contents for themselves. Mackie took immediate and effective measures against the culprits to prevent pilfering of any future supply drops. The penalties imposed by the Army included a combination of physical punishment, destruction of property, and monetary compensation.

Mackie's action was severely criticized by several of the plantation owners who had nothing better to do with their time. Fred Archer, in particular, attempted to intimidate the AIF and created a great deal of friction and animosity between the Army and the civilians. Normally, Lieutenant Mackie's conduct could not be condoned—but these were not normal times. Significantly, the local missionaries, who were always ready to side with the Europeans, kept quiet about the whole affair.

Meanwhile, around the immediate vicinity of Buka Passage, the native situation remained stable. In the south, Mason had not yet begun to feel the pressure of the pro-Japanese element. However, Paul did experience a few tenuous moments when enemy patrols—unaware of his location—ventured a bit too close for comfort. All things considered, however, coast watching in Bougainville was making progress.

Vague threats continued to filter through the Passage to the effect that the Sohano garrison would soon be on our trail. Although a large schooner was spotted moving slowly down the coast, which gave us room for speculation, it proved to be only another detachment of Japanese troops on one of their usual looting expeditions.

During the first few days of October, our teleradio transmitter began giving us trouble. Our voice circuit would not operate properly, but Mackie managed to put the telegraph key in working order just in time for Signalman Sly to tap out a report of 66 enemy aircraft racing toward Guadalcanal.

Station BTU had a busy time of it in October. Japanese aerial activity reached its peak about the middle of the month, but then it began to wane—as far as the Buka Passage was concerned. This was due mainly to the fact that the enemy had established a shore facility near Buin and had shipped in a gang of coolie laborers to construct an airfield at Kahili. Heavier and more frequent Allied bombing raids in the Passage also contributed to the Japanese strategy of building an air base at the southern tip of the island.

On October 10, 1942, I was greatly surprised to hear, over the Australian Broadcasting Network, that Mason and I had been awarded the American Distinguished Service Cross in recognition of our contribution to the war effort during the past month. But we never had a chance to savor the taste of publicity. The conflict was running like a steam roller—out of control—with Bougainville in the middle.

A couple of days later, a formation of six Flying Fortresses carried out a daylight raid on the Buka airstrip, destroying several planes on the ground and blasting a large fuel dump. Two Zeros took off in a mock attempt to intercept the bombers, but the Japs kept out of gun range.

On the night of October 16, a very heavy high-altitude attack pummeled the airfield. The entire target area was a blazing inferno of planes, gasoline, and warehouses. At that time, I had estimated that at least 50 fighter aircraft were stationed at

Buka. According to native reports, most of those planes went up in flames.

Japanese shipping in and around the Passage was negligible in comparison with that in the Buin-Faisi region. Nevertheless, our reports of enemy vessels were valuable, as information emulating from any coast watching post in enemy-occupied territory was a firsthand report.

The Japanese were well aware that an AIF detachment was hiding somewhere in the mountains and that I was operating a teleradio. They told as much to Father McConville, who was now imprisoned at Tarlena. Although he was carefully watched, McConville managed to sneak a couple of notes out to me by a trustworthy native. The enemy also knew that my call sign was BTU and that aircraft were visiting us regularly to drop parachutes.

It is rather humorous that the Japs had the idea we were being reinforced by paratroops, but the fact that they were dubious of our strength may have been the reason they were holding off coming after us.

During the month, Toshiro and a raiding party again landed at Kieta. Toshiro informed the missionaries to send word to me and the AIF soldiers to give ourselves up within a specified time or else we would be shot on sight.

I heard that four missionaries of the Marist Order—two of them women—had been executed by the Japanese on Guadalcanal. At Buin, Father Schank, along with some Sisters, were interned near the Kahili airfield, directly in the target area of Allied bombers.

About this time, Bishop Wade came out of hiding and visited the Tinputz-Raua vicinity. I did not meet him, but he sent me a letter. In the correspondence, Wade discounted my fears for the civilians. He believed that my concern for the Europeans, and especially the women, was exaggerated. He stated that those of his people who had contacted the Japanese had not been mistreated.

Wade, however, was not aware of the Guadalcanal atrocities or of the imprisonment of missionaries at Kahili. The tone of the bishop's letter was not boastful—but, rather, the expression of a man inwardly doubtful as to the wisdom of his decision. He seemed to be vainly reaching out for some grounds to convince himself that he was doing the right thing. The theme of his message dated back to our discussion of pre-occupation days, when I unsuccessfully urged him to order his people, especially the Sisters, to move inland from the beach.

In my reply, I informed Wade of the latest news. Only then did the bishop realize that, although he had banked on Japanese respect for the Church and its women, he had lost.

Wade immediately absolved the members of his mission from any further obligation to remain at their posts, but by then it was too late for most of them. The bishop begged me to do everything in my power to get the women out of Bougainville. I gave him my assurance that I would try, and I sent the following dispatch to stations VIG and KEN:

> Urgently request all possible consideration to the evacuation of about 20 women comprising the Roman Catholic Mission, and mesdames Falkner, Huson, and Campbell. In view of atrocities at Guadalcanal and elsewhere, and the improper treatment of some Sisters now interned at Kahili, I have grave fear for the safety of others. I can secretly assemble 13 women in five days or 20 in a fortnight. Teop and Numa Numa are both enemy free. Either harbor suitable for flying boats. Please advise prospects. Urgent! I repeat. Urgent!

For the better part of October, we had a bird's-eye view of an enemy survey vessel as it made a detailed exploration of Matchin Bay and the various channels along the west coast of Buka. Japanese flags were posted as markers on most of the islands and atolls in the area.

The Saposa Island people, who at the time were staunchly anti-Japanese, caused a great deal of consternation to the survey parties. Under cover of night, the natives continually removed the objectionable banners. They even forwarded a couple of the flags to me at Porapora. The Saposans had always been a renegade lot—possessed of plenty of initiative. They retrieved several bombs, which had been dumped in the sea near Soraken, and succeeded in using the explosive components to dynamite fish. For their audacity in removing the flags, a Japanese detachment staged a pre-dawn raid on Saposa—but the cunning natives had already fled to the Bougainville mainland.

On the night of October 27, another shipment of supplies was dropped for us at Rugen. This time two Catalinas were used. While one of the aircraft made its run over the clearing, the other sent a few bombs into targets on the Passage, and vice versa.

Incidentally, one of the 32 packages we picked up that night was for Mr. and Mrs. Campbell from their daughter, Nori. I believe she worked in some capacity at intelligence headquarters in Townsville. The reason this matter was brought to mind was the fact that the plantation owners—of whom the Campbells were the loudest—continued to heckle me because the authorities would not send stores to them. However, after each drop, Lieutenant Mackie, even though he had 25 men to feed, would always share his provisions with the civilians. Sugar, tea, flour, and other items were delivered to the plantations. This was a dangerous undertaking—often through enemy lines. However, instead of eliciting thanks, the shipments only whetted the public appetite for more.

CHAPTER 6

Porapora Days and the U.S.S. *Nautilus* Rescue

NOVEMBER 4, 1942–JANUARY 1, 1943

Jack Read

During the month of November 1942, aerial and marine activity at Buka Passage dwindled considerably. The airstrip had fallen into temporary disuse as a fighter base and had become a salvage and repair depot for damaged planes returning from the south. Bombers, pausing over Buka to pick up their Zero escorts, had ceased. Shipping that frequented the Passage unloaded large quantities of supplies and equipment. Fuel and ammunition dumps were established, and a number of coastal gun emplacements were erected. All kinds of construction materials were piled up on the docks. Railroad tracks were built, and rolling stock soon arrived. Tractors and lorries were unloaded at the wharves, and the garrison at Sohano was further increased.

Mason's reports of Japanese activity in the Buin area were along the same line, but on a much larger scale. Additional troop buildup was also noticed at Kieta. The enemy's strategy on Bougainville had changed to a defensive posture.

For several weeks we had heard rumors to the effect that a crack Japanese unit was due in from Rabaul to hunt us down. Then, about the first of November, my native spotters sent word that this outfit had finally arrived and would soon be on the job.

On the afternoon of November 4, Usaia's scouts counted about a hundred soldiers disembarking from a schooner anchored at Soraken. At first, I thought there was nothing unusual about this report, as Soraken was a frequent stopover for enemy military forces—especially when there was heavy traffic at the Passage.

As a precautionary measure, I had instructed Usaia Sotutu and his men to watch out for the color of the uniform worn by the Japs, which was usually all white. [Of course, the Japanese would not venture into the jungle dressed in bright white clothing.] This particular gang was clad in black. Each man carried a pack and a rifle. The soldiers were followed by a long line of dark-skinned natives carrying supplies. They certainly looked like an African safari of big game hunters—only this time, the menu was undoubtedly coast watchers. We were fortunate, however, that Porapora was a couple of hours hard climb from Soraken, and our scouts could be depended on to warn us of any immediate danger.

The teleradio was definitely the objective of this task force. As the enemy detachment moved from village to village, the inhabitants fled into the bush. A few natives, who were unable to dodge the Japs, shielded us and misled them—telling the soldiers that they had no knowledge of the AIF party or of any trails leading into the uninhabited mountain range behind Soraken.

I have always maintained, and still do, that the Japanese were never any menace to our coast watching activities. We could hide in the jungle, with perfect safety, within a few yards of them. They were not trackers. However, it became a different proposition when the enemy gained the allegiance of natives who really knew the island and who could read the telltale tracks of our every movement like an open book.

Although the Soraken people were on our side, this was mainly due to the pro-British influence of Usaia Sotutu, who was continually moving about among them. There were a couple of local natives, however, whom I did not trust, and two days later I deemed it prudent to move my men and equipment to Corporal Dolby's camp behind Aravia.

The Japanese remained in the Soraken area for a week, combing every village, campsite, and path—but they did not succeed in locating Porapora. The frustrated enemy troops returned to their schooner and headed for Sohano, threatening to shoot Usaia and his followers on sight. They also passed the word that a three-pronged drive would soon be launched against us from Baniu, Soraken, and Kunua. One would have thought that they were facing a formidable army.

Lieutenant Mackie and I held a conference concerning our future plans. The narrow stretch of country from Porapora to Aravia, and from Rugen down to the Ramasan Valley, had become too widely known as our habitat and the enemy was gradually tightening a noose around the area. In order to be of maximum value, it was necessary for Station BTU to operate from Porapora, but the station's existence threatened to be shortlived unless we could reduce our visibility.

As a result of our discussion, Mackie decided to move his men farther south and away from the vicinity of Aravia. He intended to explore the territory between Teop and Numa Numa for a new AIF base, and also to locate a new drop site to take the place of the one at Rugen. This move was calculated to give the BTU people a better chance of carrying on unmolested at Porapora.

With the Japanese still trying to snoop us out, I needed another soldier in addition to Sly. Mackie assigned Private Neil Thompson to my party. I now felt that my group was strong enough to guard against enemy surprise—and yet, at the same time, we were a mobile team.

A recent innovation in our operational procedure was the reporting of local weather conditions as they might affect Allied flight operations. I signaled stations KEN and VIG three times a day. Thus, apart from our other value, both BTU [Read] and LQK [Mason]—became advance meteorological posts, affording daily information on flying weather inside enemy lines.

One of our main concerns was the fate of the Marist missionaries being held in virtual captivity at Tarlena. A trusted native had brought a verbal message from Father McConville warning me not to attempt any communication with him. His movements were now closely watched, and spies were everywhere. McConville had just been released from temporary detention at Sohano. Both he and Laurie Chan had been forced to appear before a military court to answer charges of having furnished me with information.

Father Lebel had also been busy. On November 10, he showed up at Aravia and advised us that 11 Sisters, plus mesdames Campbell, Falkner, and Huson, were all conveniently located in case an evacuation ever became a reality. I returned to Porapora on the 15th and sent a follow-up signal to VIG and KEN regarding my original rescue request.

Mackie and I had discussed the civilian problem. We believed that although Father McConville was probably ready to risk an escape, he was handicapped by the elderly Sisters and by Fathers Morelle and Alotte, who were interned with him at Tarlena.

Usaia informed me that he approached both McConville and Laurie Chan as to the possibility of sneaking the missionaries away from the village at night and using canoes to take them to Kunua. However, the captives doubted such a plan would be successful, and they were not prepared to take the consequences of recapture by the Japanese.

The next time I saw Father Lebel was at Rugen on the morning of November 24. We were expecting our final air drop at this location on the following day. Lebel was preparing to leave immediately for Tarlena. He was determined to rescue the missionaries and anticipated reaching Tarlena soon after nightfall. He planned to leave there as soon as possible with the escapees and to return to Rugen before dawn.

The journey from Rugen to Tarlena is a long, hard, dawn-to-dusk hike. And only those who have actually experienced the difficulties of a monotonous night-long trudge through the dripping jungle can realize what lay ahead of Father Lebel.

Furthermore, in addition to the arduous trip, Lebel's scheme hinged entirely on conditions in and around the village. He would be moving secretly in the midst of disloyal natives and the Japanese themselves. I sent Corporal Sali and some of my best police boys with Father Lebel and assigned several sturdy natives to go along in case any of the elderly needed help. The spunky expedition left Rugen to tackle a task too Herculean for mere words to describe.

Miraculously the escape plan worked perfectly. The rescue team sneaked into Tarlena unobserved and left an hour later without mishap. At dusk the next day, Lebel and his weary party arrived back at Rugen. It was quite an assemblage—larger than I had anticipated. The liberated group comprised Fathers McConville, Morelle, and Alotte, three Sisters, and the half-caste Pitt family.

So far so good, but it was only logical to expect some kind of retaliation by the Japanese. On the assumption that reprisals would follow sooner rather than later, the Sisters were sheltered in the hills behind Tinputz.

We now had 17 women ready for immediate evacuation, but approval for the venture seemed to be as remote as ever. I sent another message to Mackenzie: "To avoid probable mistreatment, several missionaries and half-castes have just escaped from Tarlena to comparative safety. We are awaiting Japanese reaction. About 17 women ready in case evacuation approved." I received quick action from this last request, and chances for a rescue operation began to look good. I was advised that the airforce favored putting a flying boat down at Raua Bay, provided the location was enemy-free. I replied that, from our point of view, the Raua area was suitable in every way.

I questioned Father McConville about any information he may have gathered. But, although he had lived in close contact with the Japanese for many months, he had very little to report. This was due to the fact that his movements were confined to Tarlena. What McConville was able to tell me merely confirmed what my scouts had already described.

Very strong enemy troop concentrations existed in the vicinity of the Buka airfield and Bonis. Most of the soldiers were poorly clothed and appeared undernourished. The airstrip was littered with wrecked planes destroyed by our raids and with discarded parts of aircraft that had suffered combat damage.

Allied bombing of the Passage inflicted heavy casualties on Japanese personnel, and the enemy openly expressed fear of the Flying Fortresses. Their attitude of arrogance, displayed before the Americans invaded Guadalcanal, had been replaced by one of grave concern. The Japanese seemed to justify losing the British Solomons by circulating the story that those small islands were never much good anyway.

However, the enemy High Command declared that Bougainville was the pick of all the Solomons, that it would be adequately defended, and that U.S. forces could never get past the Japanese naval base at Buin.

In December 1942, the Buka airfield was further improved, and a prepared runway with a bitumen surface was laid down. A large electrical power plant was installed, underground fuel tanks were constructed, pillboxes were built, and trenches were reinforced. Every activity was based on defense. The airstrip remained active, but more as a beehive of industry than as a center for aircraft concentration. Single planes were observed flying all day long to and from Buin.

One feature, noticed for the first time this month, was the enemy's practice of flying night patrols during the period of the full moon. Two bombers would take off from Buka, scout up and down the east and west coasts of Bougainville, then return when the moon waned. Father McConville confirmed the Japanese assumption that Allied paratroopers were landing in the jungle. We believe that the object of these nightly searches was to intercept the Catalinas that were actually bringing in our supplies.

Another daily habit, now in vogue at Buka, was the early morning departure of two bombers. The planes flew south, one down each coast, and returned in the late afternoon. They seemed to be on a regular reconnaissance schedule. I reported these aircraft movements in detail to headquarters.

Enemy shipping around the Passage remained light. Early in the month, Mason reported a concentration of 22 ships in the Buin vicinity. I heard very little from him thereafter. Besides having trouble with his teleradio receiver, he was forced to keep moving by Japanese patrols.

The only large enemy flight passing Porapora in December occurred on the evening of the 20th. Several squadrons roared overhead going in a southeast direction. A signal was immediately flashed to Station KEN. They were bombers, probably intent on carrying out a night raid against Guadalcanal.

As the holiday season approached, Lieutenant Mackie requested that each of his men be permitted to send a Christmas greeting home. Several of the civilians made similar appeals. I reluctantly had to refuse. To have acceded would have entailed the transmission of more than 50 separate messages. We were in enemy-occupied territory, and, for security reasons, my instructions were to cut transmissions to a minimum. My duty was to preserve the teleradio for essential coast watching reports only.

However, in order to keep everybody happy, I advised VIG of my intention to add, at the end of each signal, a few names of AIF personnel until the list was complete of all Mackie's men who were alive and well. I requested Lieutenant Commander Feldt to notify their families.

On the night of December 22, the Japanese staged a surprise raid on the Raua Plantation. The enemy force, traveling by schooner and barge, entered Raua Bay in the early hours of the morning. Mr. Campbell had taken the precaution of posting several of his native boys to stand vigil day and night. He was warned of the landing, but with practically no time to spare. The Japanese disembarked at the head of the bay and moved quickly toward the plantation house. The Campbells barely escaped. They headed into the hills where Mr. Campbell had established an emergency refuge.

The Japanese attack on Raua was no coincidence. A guide, accompanying the enemy patrol, was a Buka Island native formerly employed by the Campbells as a servant. It was common knowledge that Mr. Campbell had flogged him a few days previously. The lad felt that he had been unjustly treated and immediately cleared out. To seek revenge on his employer, the native reported the incident to the Japanese and offered to guide them to the plantation.

The enemy soldiers looted and burned every building in sight. Then, at daylight, they moved out in pursuit of the couple. Meanwhile, the Campbells had reached the refuge and considered themselves safe. Their hiding place was scarcely an hour from the beach and not far from Rugen. Warned once again that the Japanese patrol was approaching, Campbell and his wife had to leave fast. They scrambled down into the Ramasan Valley where they came across Father Lebel. He guided them on the rugged trek up the valley to the former Army base at Matahai.

On December 23, while the enemy was still searching the Raua-Rugen area, Father Lebel visited me at Porapora. He argued that, as a U.S. citizen, he had a right to petition the U.S. authorities in the Solomons to evacuate their subjects— especially because most members of the Marist Order on Bougainville were Americans. I agreed, and secured permission from Lieutenant Commander Feldt to send a request to the U.S. Command at Guadalcanal.

The Japanese continued the chase and headed farther inland until they reached Namkario. An elderly native by the name of Kop was the *tul-tul* of the village. The inhabitants had fled, but Kop stood his ground and greeted the enemy soldiers. He hoped that by doing so he might save his village from destruction—for such was the Japanese method of retribution against natives who avoided them.

Kop later informed me that this enemy detachment was accompanied by Laurie Chan, who was acting as interpreter. The *tul-tul* was asked several questions, including the whereabouts of the Australian soldiers. Chan cleverly made sure that whatever question he asked during the interrogation was answered with a negative response. In a loud, domineering voice the Chinaman would shout in Pidgin English: "In what part of the bush are the Australian soldiers? You must tell the truth. You must not lie to us!" However, before Kop was able to reply, Chan added in a low whisper, apparently unintelligible to the Japs: "You must say that you do not know."

Kop got away with a noncommittal answer to every question, and saved his village in the bargain. The enemy patrol returned to Raua and then headed back to the Passage. But, before they left, Laurie Chan sneaked a warning to the *tul-tul*: "Tell the Australian soldiers to be very careful and maintain a good watch, as the Japanese are seeking them. The Japs are no good."

By late December, the AIF had established their new headquarters near the village of Namatoa—about 2,000 feet up in the mountains overlooking Teop Harbor. An auxiliary camp was kept behind the Inus Plantation to be used as a supply drop site.

We were still in pretty good shape as far as the native situation was concerned, although we noticed some infiltration by the pro-Japanese element beyond the immediate vicinity of the Buka Passage. The villages along the east coast of Bougainville, as far south as Ruri, were all beginning to waver, as were the natives in the Soraken area. I realized that my propaganda could not hope to hold them forever.

One native chieftain after another succumbed to the novelty of reporting at Sohano, where they were given a special armband—the Japanese insignia of their rank. We received a bit of a setback when the elderly chief of Ruri, always a staunchly loyal community, suddenly appeared among his people wearing the enemy armband. The natives of the village ostracized him, and he died a week later—presumably of natural causes. It is definitely within the realm of possibility that the old man, imbued with the stigma of banishment by his own people, willed himself to death. This faculty of the superstitious natives is well known in the islands.

I promptly seized the opportunity to pound another nail into the plank of my propaganda platform: "The Ruri chief died under the curse of the Japanese armband!" It helped to stem the pro-Japanese fervor, but not for long.

On Christmas Day, the enemy was again back in force along the coast from Baniu Bay to Teop. The few residents still on the beach took to the jungle. Lieutenant Mackie and his men stood by to afford whatever protection they could to the women concentrated in the hills behind Tinputz. Fortunately, the Japanese did not venture inland. The enemy soldiers packed their schooners and barges with all the livestock and produce they could lay their hands on and returned to the Passage. Nevertheless, the noose was tightening around our necks.

I had heard nothing further from Mackenzie about my request for a rescue operation. I realized that aircraft and submarines were in heavy demand and that the fate of a few people in Bougainville could not detract from Allied plans as a whole. However, it was essential that some kind of decision be made. If headquarters intended to evacuate the women, then it should be done without delay. If not, then it was up to us to move them to the most inaccessible and safest spot in the interior of the island.

Finally, on December 28, I received a signal from Station KEN, asking me to name a site, enemy free and suitable for either a flying boat or submarine. After the incident at Raua, I decided on Teop Harbor. Mackenzie advised that he was endeavoring to have a submarine detailed for the rescue attempt, but it would take a week for the ship to arrive. Furthermore, if the evacuees were unable to hang on for that length of time, arrangements would be made for a Catalina to lift them immediately. It was my opinion that the women could dodge the Japs for another week, so I opted for the submarine.

The following day, in the midst of these negotiations, KEN suddenly sprang a surprise on me. I was notified that a U.S. submarine, then scouting the coast of Buka, would attempt the evacuation that very night. Mackenzie had obviously overlooked the fact that I was located two long days to the northwest of Teop Harbor. It was impossible for me to reach Teop before the last day of the month. We agreed to hold everything in abeyance until I could establish communication with Guadalcanal direct from the rescue site.

Early on the morning of December 30, Signalman Sly and I, along with our native carriers and the teleradio, began the long, hard trek to the coast. Thompson had left a few days earlier to attend the supply drop at Inus.

However, this was not to be our lucky day. No sooner had we departed Porapora than the rain fell in torrents—as it can only do in the tropics. We made Aravia about midday, sopping wet. After a slipshod meal with a cup of tea, we sloshed through the slush toward Rugen. It was dark by the time we reached a mission shelter adjoining the plantation. We were weary, water-soaked, and hungry, so we decided to call it a day and camped for the night. Traveling as light as possible, so as not to overburden the carriers, we had not bothered to take netting or bedding along, and we cursed the discomfort and mosquitoes that robbed us of badly needed sleep.

The next day dawned bright and clear, although the heavy downpour had turned the trail into a slippery mush and made the swollen creeks and rivers difficult to ford. We tramped, stumbled, and slipped our way down to the Ramasan Valley. The Ramasan River was high, and a couple of hours elapsed before our party made it safely across with the equipment intact. My one and only transmitter nearly came to grief. A large log, racing with the current, barged into the lads carrying the teleradio. A couple of the boys were swept off their feet. But by superhuman effort the other natives reached the opposite bank with the apparatus still above water.

Climbing out of the Ramasan Valley, we trudged past the small settlement at Bukapa and plodded slowly toward Tebuin. Somewhere between the two villages we came across Father Lebel. Before we left Porapora, I had sent a runner with a message for him to meet us on the trail. Lebel informed me that the Japanese had landed at Tinputz and the Sisters were in hiding waiting for his return. I urged him to get the women on the road to Teop immediately because the evacuation would probably take place at nightfall.

The most serious difficulty we were up against was the secrecy of movement and the comparative immobility of a large group of elderly people. There was no doubt that they were feeling the strain from being on the run, and there were still several hours of rugged journey ahead of them.

I had taken every possible precaution. Police boys were posted from Baniu Bay to Teopasina. Warnings were to be signaled of any enemy intrusion. Lieutenant Mackie and his men were standing by, ready to act in case of an emergency.

A message was dispatched to the Campbells, and they were believed to be on their way from Matahai. Their journey would be a rough ten-hour trip for a young person, and Mr. and Mrs. Campbell were well past their prime in that respect. I also sent a runner down the coast to Numa Numa, in hopes that Alf Long and Max Babbage might reach Teop before the sub arrived. Eric Guthrie, Fred Archer, and Fred Urban were already in the vicinity.

By noon on the 31st, my party had reached the village of Tasku, about an hour inland from the rescue site on the foreshore of the Tearouki Plantation. I decided to set up the teleradio at Tasku. I was reluctant to move the wireless any nearer the beach in case trouble arose, necessitating a fast getaway.

I quickly established communication with KEN and was notified that negotiations were in progress for an evacuation attempt to be made about midnight. Lieutenant Mackie proceeded to the beach with several of his men. His job was to make arrangements for canoes to be in readiness and to hoist a white sheet in the trees as a signal for the submarine that was submerged somewhere out in the bay. I remained with the teleradio, keeping in constant touch with Mackenzie to await final confirmation of the operation.

Father Lebel arrived at Tasku about dusk with his travel-weary companions. The evacuees included Mrs. Huson, 14 Sisters, the elderly priests, and three young girls of the Pitt family. Friendly natives had carried several of the Sisters on improvised stretchers. Minutes later, a runner showed up with news that the Campbells would reach Tasku in a few hours. Several servants were traveling with them toting Mrs. Campbell's luggage. Alf Long and Max Babbage were already at the beach, having covered the 40 miles from Numa Numa by canoe.

Incidentally, as far as the men were concerned, their fate hung in the balance. This mission was ostensibly to rescue the women. The only male I absolutely was determined to get off my hands was Fred Urban, and he was not very cooperative. It was a much subdued Urban who had a last-minute request to me not to send him off the island as he feared possible internment in Australia. But his future on Bougainville had been decided long ago. Whether any of the other men could be accommodated aboard the submarine would be entirely at the discretion of the ship's captain.

Father Lebel wished to leave if possible. Bishop Wade had advised him to accompany the Sisters. However, although I hated to lose the priest, I also did not want to hold him against his will or the instructions from his superior. He was the only civilian with us who had a practical knowledge of emergency medical treatment. I discussed our dilemma with Lebel, and he agreed to remain on Bougainville.

About 8 P.M., I received final word from Mackenzie that we could go ahead with the evacuation. I was ordered to light a fire at 10 P.M. as a guide for the submarine and, at frequent intervals, to flash a certain Morse code signal.

In silent procession the Sisters, dressed in their flowing robes, headed for the beach. They deeply appreciated everything that was being done on their behalf. I admired the women as they waded through mud and water, stumbling over treacherous logs in the uncertain flicker of a hurricane lamp, and yet with never a murmur of complaint.

Our plans were going along as scheduled, except that there was no word from the Campbells. Father Lebel, knowing that they must be near Tasku, volunteered to go search for them. Meanwhile, I hurried to the rescue site.

Lieutenant Mackie had accomplished his mission on the shore. Canoes and paddlers were assembled. Sergeant Yauwika supervised the preparation of a fire-stack—ready to light at the appointed hour. And Signalman Sly was standing by to use the flash lamp.

Just as I was beginning to relax, and had remarked to myself how smoothly the rescue operation was proceeding, Mrs. Falkner suddenly became a problem. Despite my insistence, she flatly refused to leave the Tearouki Plantation. However, I was equally stubborn. I had worked too hard on this project to remove all the nonnative women from the island. Furthermore, I had no intention of being handicapped in the future by having Mrs. Falkner on my hands. The hour was getting late, and I had no alternative but to inform the lady that if she did not go voluntarily, she would be forcibly carried aboard the submarine. Fortunately she decided to obey my orders.

While this latest hassle was taking place, Father Lebel showed up with word that the Campbells were on their way, but moving very slowly as they were fatigued. It was now after 10 P.M., and there was a distinct possibility that they would not arrive in time.

Corporal Dolby quickly came to our aid. He and Private Waterhouse volunteered to go back with a team of natives in order to help the couple along. The Campbells reached the evacuation site within the hour, although Dolby later informed me that he had had to be harsh to the point of rudeness to impress upon them the need for haste.

My first intimation of the submarine's presence came at midnight. I heard a voice faintly hailing out of the darkness. I immediately jumped in a canoe and paddled across the harbor to investigate. A few hundred yards from shore, I came upon a small launch towing a rubber raft. The boat was manned by Lieutenant Richard Lynch and chief petty officers Red Porterfield and Moe Killgore of the U.S.S. *Nautilus*. Their craft was jammed on a reef and shipping water. Lieutenant Lynch said that the submarine was standing off a few miles out in the bay.

I raced back to shore for help, and in a short time, with native muscle, we pulled the launch off the reef. Luckily no material damage had been done. The boat's crew reminded me that we were just entering the New Year of 1943. I was invited to join them and honor the occasion in the good old traditional manner. And we did, right in the middle of Teop Harbor with a bottle of medicinal brandy. Then it was back to the business at hand.

I explained our situation to Lieutenant Lynch. His instructions were to pick up only 17 women. The three Pitt girls and nine men would be an addition to the expected quota. We knew that it would be necessary for the launch to make a second trip if the entire group was to be rescued. A complete evacuation depended on whether the sub's skipper, Commander William Brockman, had room on his ship for everybody. There was also a time factor to be considered. Another round-trip by the boat would entail some delay, and Brockman wanted to be clear of Bougainville by daybreak.

Lieutenant Lynch and I worked out an arrangement. The women would leave first. The men would follow in canoes, as far out in the bay as safety permitted, then wait for the launch to return and pick them up. The craft would only come back subject to Commander Brockman's approval. It was also essential that the evacuees take with them the absolute minimum of baggage—no more than what they could actually carry.

The launch followed me back to shore. It was jam-packed with supplies I had requested from Mackenzie, including medical stores, emergency rations, binoculars, pistols, tommy guns, walkie-talkies, and six-volt lead acid batteries. Lieutenant Lynch and his men also carried presents from the crew of the submarine—several cartons of cigarettes, tins of tobacco, matches, clothing, toilet articles, and other items. The gifts were unexpected and very much appreciated.

By the time we arrived at the beach, Mackie had canoes in the water and paddlers standing by. The women and girls were rapidly assembled and assigned to the launch.

However, once again the spotlight centered around the Campbells. Their servants had followed them with a large amount of baggage. Mrs. Campbell insisted that it all had to go. She was not leaving anything behind. My protests were to no avail. I left the decision up to Lieutenant Lynch, but he was also unable to reason with the lady. Therefore, on its first trip, the launch was crowded with not only the women and girls, but the Campbell's luggage as well. However, that was not our only surprise. During the confusion of loading, Mr. Campbell had somehow squeezed himself aboard without being noticed. To say that the craft was riding low in the water would be a whopping understatement.

I accompanied the canoes carrying the remaining eight men out about two miles from shore. We sat drifting and waiting for the boat to return. An hour or so dragged by and it seemed that Commander Brockman's decision had gone against us. At 4 A.M., I was just about ready to give up hope, when our natives, with their keen ears, heard the craft heading in toward us. Time was now more precious than ever. The evacuees were speedily transferred to the launch. We waved them farewell as Lieutenant Lynch swung his boat about and aimed for the open sea and safety.

We had no sooner dragged our canoes back up on the beach at Teop than the first light of New Year's Day 1943 began to crest over the eastern horizon. I felt extremely relieved of a huge responsibility. Nevertheless, the sudden departure of so many important residents tended to cast a shadow of gloom over our future. I noticed the natives meandering along the shore in small groups, talking among themselves in whispered conversation.

For the past year, I had managed to hold together a large populated area of the island by propaganda methods that were now becoming a bit stale. The natives began questioning the evacuation. They asked: "Why should our plantation employers and the missionaries flee Bougainville if American forces are about to drive the Japanese from the island? Are the Japanese, and their native followers, telling the truth—that the war is over and that they were victorious?"

I was impelled to keep inventing new propaganda tactics to counter every delicate situation that arose and to take advantage of every opportunity to remove the doubts of the native population. Coast watching on Bougainville depended on our ability of persuasion.

We were back at Tasku shortly after daybreak, and I signaled KEN that the evacuation had been accomplished without a hitch.

However, the operation was marred in one dangerous aspect: the lack of censorship of news items before they were released. Soon after the evacuees landed at Guadalcanal, the whole world knew about the feat. The broadcasting networks flooded the airways with accounts of a daring submarine that had rescued 29 civilians from Bougainville. The complete story of the expedition was reported—with the exception of mentioning Teop Harbor. I was tempted to send Mackenzie a message of protest, but the damage had already been done. The Japs would now certainly be on our trail—and hopping mad.

CHAPTER 7

Missionary Work on Buka and Bougainville and the U.S.S. *Nautilus* Rescue

SEPTEMBER 1940–JANUARY 4, 1943

Sister Mary Irene Alton

During the summer of 1940, Marist Bishop Thomas Wade was in urgent need of two teachers and a couple of registered nurses for missionary work in his district of the northern Solomon Islands.

Forty Sisters volunteered for the assignment, and four were selected from the Sisters of St. Joseph of Orange, California. Sisters Mary Irene Alton and Mary Hedda Jaeger were trained nurses, while Sisters Mary Isabelle Aubin and Mary Celestine Belanger were teachers. In September 1940, the four chosen missionaries, and Mother Frances Lirette, sailed from San Pedro, California, aboard the steamer Mariposa.

Following is Sister Mary Irene Alton's description of the missionary activities on Buka and Bougainville Islands and of the eventual evacuation of the missionaries.

We landed in Sydney, Australia, where we waited for a small cargo ship to take us north to the Solomons. Upon reaching our destination, Buka Island, we met the Marist Priests and Sisters. They had been working in this area of the world for many years and were able to acquaint us with our new tasks and life in the tropics. Mother Frances remained with us for a month, until we got settled, and then she returned to the United States.

Our duties included teaching the natives and nursing their sick. At first, the women and children of the villages were afraid of us and would run into the jungle when we attempted to treat them. But after learning that our nursing and medicines could cure their tropical ailments, they began coming willingly to the dispensary for help.

The birthrate among these primitive people was tremendous. Whenever twins were born to a family, the firstborn was kept, and the second child was either drowned or disposed of. This practice made our job as missionaries very difficult— teaching the importance of a soul.

[The bombing of Pearl Harbor, and the rapid Japanese advance across the South Pacific, rudely interrupted the dedicated work of the Solomon Island missionaries.]

We were well aware of the proximity of the enemy because of events that were occurring. The Japanese had killed our Australian neighbor, Mr. Good. He had a radio and was able to send messages to American officials in the southern Solomons.

Bishop Wade soon decided that the missionaries would be safer if they were moved to the larger island of Bougainville. Father Lebel, a Marist Priest, was appointed to take charge of us.

For the entire year of 1942, we lived, camped, and traveled from one hiding place to another—always avoiding the high mountain areas where cannibals were known to exist. The Sisters back home in Orange and our relatives could receive no word from us.

[In December 1942, the Japanese were busy occupying the eastern seaboard of Bougainville and sending out patrols to search for the Australian coast watchers and Americans. Father Lebel assembled the ten Marist Sisters and four Sisters of St. Joseph. He sadly gave them the bad news. In order to survive, it was necessary to hide out in the dangerous high country of the island.]

Our group traveled by foot into the craggy mountains of Bougainville. We endured many hardships—torrential rains, thunder, and lightning. But, the blessed rain furnished us with water for drinking, cooking, and our household and personal needs.

Our diet consisted of food generously donated by the natives—taro, wild leaves for vegetables, nuts, bananas, wild pig, and opossum. The natives added roast cats to their diet, but we did not relish this "delicacy" and did not partake of cat meat. Another deprivation was the lack of salt, sugar and flour.

[The health of the Sisters gradually began to deteriorate. At various times the missionaries suffered from malaria, dysentery, and pneumonia. Because the Americans had no way of sending messages to Guadalcanal reporting their safety, friends and relatives in the United States assumed they had died at the hands of the Japanese. Masses were even said for the "dead missionaries."

Despite the isolation and adversity, the Sisters continued with their tasks of teaching the natives and caring for the sick.]

Bishop Wade was among those who needed medical attention. And I was delegated to alleviate his pain—a molar tooth that needed extraction. I claimed lack of expertise in this field, but Bishop Wade insisted that if I did not pull the tooth, he would do it himself. I asked the Bishop to offer us his Mass for the success of the operation. Sister Isabelle acted as my assistant and held the flashlight—and prayed.

It's amazing what one can accomplish under stress and necessity. It was a successful extraction—roots and all. But during the whole time, I kept thinking about the irony of the situation: a Bishop for my first dental patient!

Later, many natives, and even Sisters, came to me for the same operation. All were done in an old hut—under the illumination of a flashlight. [On Christmas Eve 1942, Father Lebel informed the missionaries that the Japanese were nearby and methodically patrolling the east coast of Bougainville.]

Loyal natives guided us higher into the mountains. Several of the elderly Marist Sisters and Priests were carried on stretchers. We camped near a river.

[Father Lebel set out to contact the coast watchers and to arrange for the rescue of the Americans. By the time he contacted the Australians, Lebel's tennis shoes had been worn out and his feet were bloody. After the evacuation of the missionaries was approved, Father Lebel hurried back to the hideout and preparations were made for the rescue attempt.]

Father Lebel gave orders that each of us could only take one small package or bag. We were not told how the evacuation was to be effected. We assumed that it would be by plane—but we never dreamed that we would be liberated from the island by submarine.

It was night when we descended the dark jungle trails to Teop Harbor, and we had many frightening experiences while climbing down the steep mountain paths. The Australian soldiers, Father Lebel, and the natives helped us form a long, single-file procession. The natives cut through the thick jungle undergrowth and carried the weak and older Sisters on stretchers. The natives also helped us in crossing crocodile-filled rivers.

We could hear the weird jungle noises, see the flying fox, iguanas, snakes, and very large rats. One of the Sisters lost a shoe, and another dropped her package of clean clothes in a muddy river.

On the beach, the coast watchers and Father Lebel hung a large white sheet in the trees and built a fire. This was a signal for the submarine. Meanwhile, native men and young boys lined up several narrow outrigger canoes in order to meet a schooner and rubber boat from the American submarine *Nautilus*. Some of us expressed fear of falling in the ocean from the small canoes. But a young native answered in Pidgin English, "Mifella catchem you quick time." Translated, "We'll pick you up quickly."

Among the 29 people to be evacuated from Bougainville were two elderly Priests, ten Marist Sisters, our group of four Sisters of St. Joseph, some Australians, and three half-caste children—whose parents had asked us to care for them. The children could only speak Pidgin English and were barefooted. They wore little lava-lava wraparound skirts.

We were transported in two trips to the submarine. The sailors aboard the *Nautilus* had only been told that they were rescuing 14 American women. They had no idea that we were missionary Sisters. The navy men prepared to meet us by cleaning up and shaving for the occasion. I am sure that they were not only surprised—but perhaps disappointed. However, they made the best of the situation and treated us with great respect and consideration.

We reached the submarine at midnight. A number was called out for each refugee, as we took turns climbing down the hatch ladder into the ship. What a treat it was to eat bread and to indulge in such luxuries as salt, sugar, and even Christmas candy. The children were given gifts of sweaters and tennis shoes. The sailors even took up a collection for the youngsters, who were unable to communicate too well with the navy boys in Pidgin English.

After traveling on the *Nautilus* for four days, we rendezvoused with an American subchaser that was to take us to Guadalcanal. It was a very dark night, and as we climbed a rope ladder to the deck of the vessel, one could see nothing but the white of our habits and white veils. The sailors thought that sacks of flour were being carried aboard.

When we reached Guadalcanal, we were transferred to a transport, the *Hunter Liggett*, which was carrying a human cargo of wounded men to New Zealand.

[After arriving at the island, the Sisters of St. Joseph boarded the ship *West Point* for their return to the United States. The Marist Sisters and the others rescued from Bougainville remained in New Zealand.

In 1946, after the war, Sisters Mary Irene Alton and Mary Isabelle Aubin returned to the Solomons. They were accompanied by two new companions, Sister Marian Durand and Sister Bertha Vigeant.]

We started all over again, but this time we had new medicines for malaria—and penicillin for tropical ulcers and other serious diseases.

From an Army hospital, Bishop Wade received jeeps, trucks, Quonset huts, and furniture. He was also given tanks and flour drums, which could be used for collecting and storing rainwater. Roads had been made serviceable by our military—as only they can do it.

Our praise and thanksgiving to God for saving our lives, and that of the others. And our appreciation to the Navy and other servicemen—to the Australian coast watchers, who will long remain a very important part of our prayers. We know that we could never have withstood those distressing trials of life during that time, had it not been for God's gifts of faith, prayer, and trust in His Divine Providence.

CHAPTER 8

The Japanese Search for the Southern Bougainville Radio Station

AUGUST 8, 1942–JANUARY 1, 1943

Paul Mason

From the moment that U.S. forces launched their offensive in the Solomon Islands on August 7, 1942, I began sending daily reports, in plain language, of all enemy aircraft formations heading for Tulagi and Guadalcanal. During the first several days of the amphibious operation, my messages were picked up by Port Moresby, relayed to Townsville, thence to Honolulu, for further transfer to the U.S. Military Command in the Solomons.

About the 18th of August, I was instructed to send my signals directly to Mackenzie, who had established his radio station [KEN] on Guadalcanal. Because of this more efficient means of communication, Allied units in the southern Solomon Islands received timely warnings, from both Jack Read and myself, of impending air raids.

I was familiar with the area where the Americans were fighting and was able to listen in on conversations taking place between planes and their carriers. Keeping my ear glued to the radio, I learned as much about the battle going on as Guadalcanal Control did.

My coast watching base was well situated near Turiboiru, with a lookout post three miles distant at Malabita. Besides reporting enemy aircraft flights, I also signaled Japanese ship movements.

Unfortunately, at this stage of the war, I did not have any means of accurately identifying enemy warships. We had neither drawings nor silhouettes of Japanese vessels. Because of this predicament, our task was extremely difficult, especially when the number of ships in the Buin vicinity began to dramatically increase.

I sent an urgent message to Station VIG requesting sketches of known ships, but it was not until October that Lieutenant Commander Feldt air dropped several penciled silhouettes. From that point on, we were able to more accurately identify the different classes of Japanese heavy and light cruisers.

Our November supply drop included photographs of enemy vessels, which enabled us to perfect our methods of identification. However, I preferred the simple silhouettes that were printed on plain paper and could be easily set afire in an emergency. The heavy photo stock used by the U.S. Navy absorbed too much moisture in the tropics and was very hard to ignite. At a later date, I was forced to burn the photos one by one in a very hot flame in order to destroy them. I was then in very great danger and could ill afford to waste the time.

Meanwhile, getting back to the beginning of the Solomon Islands campaign, as soon as Guadalcanal was attacked, the Japs at Kieta left town in a hurry. They told the natives that they were going down to "a big fight in New Guinea."

Owing to the failure of our supply drop at the Puriata River, we were now very short of stores. A new resupply mission was arranged, and the drop took place at Barillo, about 16 miles inland from Buin. Otton and his men collected all the parachutes and had the bundles back at my headquarters early in the next morning. I received a copy of the Sydney *Bulletin*. It was the first newspaper I had seen in eight months.

Throughout the latter part of August, Japanese float planes were observed flying low concentric air searches over the coastal plain. I suspected that they were searching for us.

During this period, several large detachments of enemy soldiers continually came ashore from ships in the area. These troops seemed to be relaxing on a shore leave of some sort.

On one occasion, Japanese soldiers contacted a group of local natives near Kangu. The people thought the soldiers were looking for a crashed plane, but I believed that they were scouting the vicinity for a possible airfield. These Japs refused to allow the curious natives to follow them while they attempted to survey the open swampy terrain behind Moila Point. I began to feel uncomfortable as we were located in flat land within a few miles of the enemy troops.

After the soldiers returned to their ship, natives informed me that the Japs had planted notice-boards along several paths. I sent a couple of natives to bring one of the posters to me and had it translated. The notice listed the names of two airmen and directed them to hurry back to their vessel. I told the natives to return the notice-board and replace it exactly where they had found it. The Japanese never realized that I borrowed the poster. A short time later, the missing airmen saw the message and went back to their ship.

For several days, enemy troops continued coming ashore from the ever-increasing number of Japanese warships and transports that were anchored off Buin.

On September 9, the natives of Lanuai Village sent a delegation to our camp and asked me to shift my base of operation. They said that the Japs were bringing beds ashore and this time they meant to stay permanently. However, from our lookout post we spotted more than just beds. Tractors, lorries, heavy guns, and war material of all kinds were being unloaded. I quickly decided that this was a good time to get moving.

Accompanied by Wigley, Otton, and my native gang, I established a new post near Barougo—on the saddle that joins the Crown Prince and Deuro mountain ranges. From this spot, my field of vision extended from Toimonapu Bay, on the northeast coast, to the mouth of the Puriata River in the west. Although the spurs of the Deuro Range created a blind spot

that obscured Tonolei Harbor, I was still able to look across the
Bougainville Strait, eastward beyond Oema Island and south
over the Buin coast to the Fauro and Shortland Islands. This
was almost an ideal post, and I regretted not having used it
before. However, because the Crown Prince Range concealed,
to some extent, the approach of enemy aircraft from the
northwest, the location had its disadvantages.

Shortly after the Japanese began to consolidate their position at Buin, certain natives betrayed the missionaries and Chinese who were hiding in the hills. The Chinese were warned of
the treachery in time and just managed to escape. One group
of Orientals headed for Tom Ebery's hideout behind Toimonapu. Another party, led by Chong You, moved toward the west
coast, then doubled back across the island to join Wong You at
Korpe.

The missionaries were not so lucky. Fathers Poncelet,
Schank, and six Sisters made no attempt to flee and were captured by the Japanese. I learned that they were severely mistreated for not disclosing our coast watching activities. The
priests had also instructed the natives not to reveal my whereabouts.

In a feverish attempt to find my new base, the enemy tried
unsuccessfully to gain favor with the Buin natives, many of
whom had worked on my plantation before the war. Unlike the
Kieta and Negavisi people, the Buin tribesmen did not, at any
time, betray me. When asked my location, they would point to
the south and say, "Sydney, Sydney."

However, we still became subjected to many life-threaten-
ing situations as the Japs began foraging and patrolling inland
from the coast. One of their scouting parties, comprised of 80
soldiers on bicycles, came within a few hundred yards of our
campsite.

Throughout the month of September, the Japanese pressed
hundreds of natives into forced labor constructing an airfield
at Kahili and, of course, promising to pay them after the war. I
sent one of my native boys, Lukabai, to assist the Japs in their

"good work." Like most of the tribe people, he carried a 16-inch bush knife as his working tool. Twice a week, Lukabai returned to our base and gave a detailed progress report on the airstrip. On September 23, I sent the following message to Port Moresby:

> Aerodrome expected to be completed in ten days. Hundreds of natives used as forced labor. Many vehicles, tractors, and heavy equipment are observed. Stores and fuel dumps are camouflaged under tarpaulins spread along the shoreline from the Ugumo to Molika Rivers. Two antiaircraft batteries near mouth of the Ugumo. One antiaircraft gun at northwest boundry of airstrip. Wireless station and eight iron buildings have been built. Missionaries are interned in buildings on the beach. Enemy soldiers wear green uniforms with an anchor badge on their arm. Scouts report that Japanese troops number about 440 men.

Because of the enemy occupation of Buin, I requested that future supplies be air dropped at Toimonapu. However, we were given only a few hours notice for our next shipment. Due to heavy rains, we were unable to cross the flooded Luluai River in time to light the signal fires. I could hear the Catalina flying up and down the coast searching for the flaming fire-stacks.

The aircraft finally dropped the parachutes and bundles into the swamps near Toimonapu. A month was to elapse before we managed to recover the stores. In the meantime, we ran short of rations. The enemy was confiscating all native food in the district. I urgently asked for another drop to be made near Barillo—an hour's journey by bicycle from Kahili.

Previously, we always managed to find natives to help search for bundles after a supply mission. On this occasion, however, the Barillo people were working for the Japs at the airfield and hesitated to help us. After much haggling, I finally convinced the natives that they would be able to work for us at night and the Japs during the day. It was not until I mentioned that they would be paid for their efforts did they agree to my terms, and all supplies were then collected.

Throughout the next few months I continued to report the steady growth and development of the Japanese naval base in the Buin-Faisi-Tonolei area. We frequently sighted at least 13 cruisers and more than 35 destroyers gathered in the vicinity of the Bougainville Strait. Twelve cargo vessels, which I reported on November 10, were subsequently sunk by U.S. planes off Guadalcanal.

Although Mackenzie requested continuous news of enemy shipping movements, and the total daily number of vessels sighted, Lieutenant Commander Feldt asked me to restrict my message traffic to one signal a day, and then on only certain days of the week. I resolved the dilemma by sending occasional signals to Port Moresby and more regular transmissions to Guadalcanal. I also telegraphed Mackenzie three daily weather reports in addition to shipping and aircraft sightings.

From time to time, Lieutenant Commander Feldt sent us encouraging letters with our supplies. Because I had no personal contact with other naval officers, or any of the authorities I was working for, these messages heartened me a great deal. Mackenzie would often let Read know the score of enemy planes destroyed in the Solomons, and I was able to intercept this information. It was very encouraging to hear the results of our efforts.

Coast watchers, like Jack Read and myself, continually operated under a great amount of stress. Consequently we had a tendency to grow stale. However, when we were told something of the conflict's overall picture, our interest and incentive revived and our teamwork improved. It was not that we expected "pats on the back," but we could tackle the job with fresh enthusiasm when we knew our reports were helping the Allies score a goal or two.

In November, I was advised that I had been commissioned a sub-lieutenant in the naval volunteer reserve. Although I did not receive any additional pay, the appointment did give me a measure of satisfaction. I felt that the Royal Australian Navy had recognized my accomplishments.

By this time, the Buin area and the southeast coast of Bougainville were becoming too dangerous for the Catalinas. Therefore, I requested the December drop to be made at Ugubakogui near the Abia River.

On the afternoon of the scheduled night shipment, the chief of the Ugubakogui tribe, a good-natured but fussy little fellow, showed up at the drop site. He was very excited and told me that his people were faced with a problem. They were more than willing to help us retrieve the supplies, but a member of the tribe had died that day and it was required for the men of the village to cremate the body in a funeral pyre. This crema-tion business could become a complicated mess. What if the Catalina pilot mistook the funeral pyre for our fire-stack signal? It was already after 4 o'clock. I decided to try and negotiate with the chief and asked, "Can you cook him before the moon comes up?" He replied that he thought it could be done. I knew that the natives were at least an hour's walk to the funeral spot, so I told the chief, "Hurry up and cook him, then come to the drop site and be ready to light the signal fires."

The funeral went off like clockwork and so did our supply operation. By the next morning, the natives had carried the stores to our camp and dump locations. Everybody was happy with a job well done. The corpse was well done also.

On December 20, a tribe of about 40 natives left their east coast village near Olava and sought refuge on Rantan Island. They later returned to Bougainville and related the following account. According to their story, enemy soldiers visited them on the island and told the natives that the Sadi chief had informed the Japs that the people of Olava might know where I was located. The Japanese told the Rantan refugees that Nip-pon was now their government and that the natives could now enjoy many advantages—such as being able to drink as much whiskey as they wanted without being flogged. The Japs also threatened to annihilate the tribe if they refused to disclose our exact position. The natives refused to be taken in by this ploy and replied that if this was Japanese law, they would not live under it. They then secretly abandoned Rantan Island and moved to the banks of the Luluai River on the mainland.

Although the natives were a seafaring people, they hid in the bush—fishing in the river and working the swamp sago for a living. The vengeful tribesmen asked me to arrange to have bombs dropped on the house of the Sadi chief, where he and four other men lived with their womenfolk. The Sadi people had been armed by the Japs and agreed to help hunt us down.

I reported the incident to Mackenzie and was ordered to move my base farther inland and to maintain radio silence for a week. We traveled northwest and established a camp above Turitai. I hoped that I would still be able to cover enemy shipping and aircraft flights from the range of mountains between the Luluai Valley and the northeast coast.

We spent Christmas with Tom Ebery. During our visit, the chief of the Luluai tribe arrived and told me that the Japanese had threatened him with death if he refused to join them in searching for our camp. The chief assured me that he would rather die than give our location away. He also related information that the Taberoi Village chieftain and his *tul-tul* were urging the Japs to come after us.

I decided to keep moving and retreated over the coastal range, then across the Luluai Valley to Orimai. While at Orimai, a Fijian Methodist Mission teacher, by the name of Eroni, contacted us. He had been hiding in a village near Ebery's hideout and informed me that it had been raided by an enemy patrol. The Japs discovered several packets of mail, including letters from Read and me, and also mail belonging to the AIF soldiers. The Japs arrested several natives and Chinese, but Tom managed to escape. A couple of days prior to this raid, a Japanese party took Father Junkers and two elderly Sisters prisoner at Koromira.

The enemy appeared to be closing in on us fast. We knew that the Japs were not fond of traveling in the high country, so we elected to cross some of the roughest terrain in Bougainville—the southeast end of the Crown Prince Range. From Orimai, we made our way over the mountains to Koniguru and then headed to Tapopiso.

Meanwhile, the Japs were hot on our trail. They had been told that we were at Orimai and launched a three-pronged drive against the village. To the south, the enemy cut off Orimai from the coastal plain and sealed the northern pass at the head of the Luluai Valley. From the east, the main Japanese force, consisting of 40 soldiers and 60 Kieta natives, descended on the village and shot up our former campsite.

While we rested at Tapopiso, two Methodist Mission boys arrived with news that the Japs had captured Tom Ebery. Fearing that the enemy probably knew our location by now, we immediately backtracked toward the coast to Siuru. It was when we arrived at Siuru that I learned of the last days and death of Tom Ebery.

Ebery came to Bougainville in 1915. As a young man, he had broken his collarbone and shoulder blade in an accident and was never able to raise his right arm above his shoulder. Tom Ebery, like myself, had volunteered to serve as a civilian coast watcher. However, after Merrylees confiscated Tom's transmitter during the evacuation from Kieta, Ebery never had a real chance to share in the work that Read and I were doing.

Tom Ebery also suffered painfully from a persistent shoulder abscess that prevented him from exercising. As a result, he became very stout. However, he was still able to give us a great deal of information on enemy movements. Tom was the sort of man who helped everybody. He became a father figure to all the natives—attending to the sick and judging their arguments.

When the Japanese attacked the village near his hideout, Tom attempted to elude the enemy, but the Kieta natives tracked him down in the bush and flogged him before handing him over to the conquering soldiers of Nippon. The Japs, assuming that Ebery had knowledge of our whereabouts, took him to Kieta for interrogation. Tom, of course, knew nothing of our movements since we had seen him last. The frustrated Japanese brought the poor man back to Toimonapu. Then, in a diabolical frenzy, with sticks and bayonet thrusts, they drove him over the coastal ranges, down into the Luluai Valley and up to Orimai. After attacking the village, and finding that we had already left the area, the Japs prodded Ebery up and down the gorges of the Pirias and Abia rivers. While they were forcing Tom to cross the flooded upper reaches of the Mailai River, he collapsed and was washed downstream. Friendly local natives found the body and buried him on the riverbank.

For the past several months, the Kieta natives, who enjoyed Japanese patronage, had been given a free hand. They looted and pillaged both friendly and neutral tribes. The ravaged people said over and over again: "It is not the Jap who is bad, it is the Kieta native!"

By the end of December 1942, Japanese patrols, moving southwest from Orimai, had reached Turiboiru, where they established a permanent base.

Portrait of
Paul Mason.
COURTESY OF
NOELLE MASON

Paul Mason and Wong You. COURTESY OF NOELLE MASON

Sisters of St. Joseph of Orange, California, who were trapped on Bougainville Island. Left to right: Sister M. Irene Alton, Sister M. Hedda Jaeger, Sister M. Celestine Belanger, and Sister M. Isabelle Aubin. COURTESY OF SISTER MARY IRENE ALTON

Bishop Thomas Wade. COURTESY OF REV. GEORGE M. LEPPING, S.M.

The teleradio.

Kieta Harbor, Bougainville Island, October 10, 1942.

Japanese ships assembled in Tonolei Harbor, southern
Bougainville, October 10, 1942. COURTESY U.S. NAVY

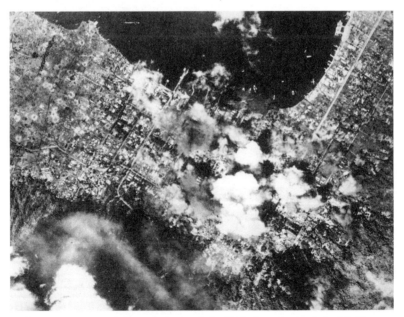

Rabaul, New Britain, under attack by U.S. bombers, July 1943.
COURTESY NATIONAL ARCHIVES

Henderson Field, Guadalcanal. COURTESY U.S. NAVY

Detachment of U.S. Marines march past a B-17 Flying Fortress on Henderson Field, Guadalcanal. Another B-17 can be seen in background. COURTESY U.S. NAVY

Japanese torpedo planes attacking American task force off Guadalcanal, August 8, 1942. Two enemy planes burn in background. COURTESY U.S. NAVY

A PBY-5 Catalina flying boat somewhere in the southwest Pacific.
COURTESY NATIONAL ARCHIVES

A PBY-5 Catalina flying boat of the type flown by the Australian Air Force. COURTESY U.S. NAVY

Sergeant
Bill Dolby.

Lieutenant
Commander
Eric Feldt.

U.S. Navy planes attack Japanese airfields on either side of the
Buka Passage, November 1, 1943. Buka airstrip can be seen to the
right, and Bonis to the left, of the photograph. COURTESY NATIONAL
ARCHIVES

CHAPTER 9

The Reorganization of the Coast Watching Operation and the U.S.S. *Gato* Rescue

JANUARY 2–APRIL 30, 1943

Jack Read

When we returned to Tasku, on New Year's Day 1943, Signalman Sly and I promised ourselves a day off. We had been going strong for more than 48 hours without sleep—and that, plus the 30-mile rugged march from Porapora to Teop, was beginning to take its toll on everybody.

We had just settled down for a nap when an excited, out-of-breath native scout rushed into the campsite. He reported that an enemy schooner had landed an armed party of about a hundred Japanese on the beach at Tearouki and they were already working their way inland. We had neither the strength nor means to oppose them and, in any case, such action was contrary to policy. We immediately packed up and got moving. Lieutenant Mackie and his detachment hurried to join the rest of their unit at Namatoa, while I headed back to Porapora with my group.

Several of the police boys, who I had posted at various points along the coast, met me at Tebuin. They reported that additional enemy landings had also been made at Baniu, Raua, and Tinputz. Japanese patrols were observed operating simultaneously from those points. This new development caused me to change my plans. Our usual route to Porapora was no longer safe for the carriers and teleradio. I decided to go into hiding somewhere while my scouts got the lay of the land.

We left the main path at Tebuin and followed a native trail through the jungle. I hoped to join Father Lebel at the refugee camp recently vacated by the Sisters. We reached the site within a couple of hours. Lebel was already there, along with Father McConville, Brother Karl, and Bobby Pitt and his wife. The Pitts were extremely thankful to me for sending three of their daughters to safety.

By this time, my men and I were exhausted. Sleep and rest could no longer be staved off. Reliable natives were posted at all possible approaches to the camp, and we turned in.

The next morning, information filtered through to the effect that all the landing parties had converged on Tinputz. Three schooners, camouflaged with shrubbery, were anchored in the harbor. The Japs were busy dismantling a sawmill plant and loading lumber, iron, and other building materials aboard the vessels. A number of Kieta natives accompanied the enemy. They were acting as pro-Japanese propaganda hucksters wherever local natives were contacted.

Having benefited from a good night's sleep, we moved into the Ramasan Valley where Neil Thompson met us with a crew of natives. They were carrying our stores, which had been dropped at Inus the night before the evacuation. Thompson reported that the drop was a success and the entire consignment of 30 packages had been recovered. Included among the supplies were several cartons of cigarettes marked "From the boys where this aircraft came from." This had become a regular feature of each drop, and the lads looked forward to these "extras." In my usual signal, advising the results of each supply mission, I always incorporated a word of thanks to the donors, whoever they were, and I trust that they were informed of our appreciation.

A fortnight had now elapsed with no signal from Mason that he was back on the air. He had been ordered to maintain radio silence for one week only. Furthermore, none of his party had shown up at a prearranged drop site where a Catalina had attempted to parachute stores to his group. Lieutenant Commander Feldt asked if a small patrol could be detailed to investigate. Mackie acted immediately on the request. Corporal McLean and a party headed south the following morning. Our anxiety was relieved when Mason was heard on the air a few days later. However, it was too late to recall McLean and his men. They continued on and eventually met up with Paul.

The Japanese remained at Tinputz for three days before embarking for Kieta. Apparently their objective had been to carry out a beach reconnaissance for construction materials and anything else that might be of value to them. After the enemy departed, we resumed the journey to Porapora and reached Lumsis the first day. Besides the Aravia natives, the people of Lumsis remained loyal to us until the very end. I decided to set up a base in the mountains behind Lumsis—a place to fall back on in case Porapora became untenable.

While we were at the village, another problem presented itself. Natives living on the island who were foreign to Bougainville—such as people from New Britain and the other islands, were known locally as "Redskins." The term derives from the fact that their pigmentation is somewhat lighter than that of the average Buka and Bougainville native. There were a hundred or so of them working in northern Bougainville when the Japanese invaded the islands. The subsequent departure of their employers left the Redskins more or less stranded, and the local natives did not want them hanging around the villages. It was a drain on the food supply and invariably became a cause of domestic strife. The people turned to me to solve their dilemma.

The Aravia and Lumsis natives were very amiable. I was able to purchase a block of fertile land from each community and settled the Redskins on the property. However, in return, I asked them to serve me as carriers or laborers whenever called upon. They willingly agreed to the proposal. Incidentally, practically all my police boys were Redskins.

I returned to Porapora on January 6. Usaia Sotutu and his men had been holding down the fort in my absence. While I was away, Allied bombers carried out, a damaging raid on the Passage. They destroyed many aircraft on the ground and knocked out a large searchlight that had just been installed. But, also during this period, shiploads of soldiers had been landed, and enemy troop concentrations were now dispersed along the shore of Matchin Bay and the west coast of Buka Island. Tarlena quickly developed into a Japanese stronghold and became the nucleus of further expansion into Chabai, Porton, and Soraken.

Now, more so than ever, I regretted the fact that I was never given permission to carry out a scorched earth policy, which I had requested to do on several occasions. Admittedly, the destruction of a few houses would only have been a drop in the bucket as far as disrupting Japanese plans. Nevertheless, the basic principle of warfare is to do anything and everything to make the enemy's job of conquest more difficult. Had this policy been adopted earlier, the Japanese would have found their task of occupation not quite so simple.

By this time, it was a bit late in the day to consider a scorched earth policy, but I was determined to make the enemy's takeover of Soraken as difficult as possible. The large number of buildings situated in the vicinity was an open invitation to Japanese forces. And, because the town was directly beneath my camp at Porapora, enemy seizure would make it a dangerous threat to my observation post.

On the night of January 10, Usaia Sotutu and Corporal Sali secretly sneaked down the mountain into Soraken and set fire to every building and wharf. At dawn, the enemy arrived in force to view the gutted ruins. We aimed to do the same to Chabai and Porton, but the plan misfired. However, I am convinced that our action delayed the Japanese occupation of Soraken.

Early in January, the native situation began to take a turn for the worse. The people of Ruri really believed my propaganda that the death of their chief was caused by his wearing the armband of Nippon. They spread the story far and wide, and consequently many Japanese armbands were thrown away.

The natives of Sorem Village, three miles south of the Passage, were very much pro-Japanese. They considered themselves very important people. They fraternized and drank whiskey with the Japs and were gullible to enemy promises of intermarriage after the war was over. Enticements such as these were standard Japanese methods of currying native favor.

The Sorem residents lured several Ruri men to their village, where they were captured and turned over to the Japanese as being pro-British. The prisoners were flogged and interned at the Passage. I quickly realized that unless this sort of thing was stopped, the Japanese sphere of influence would grow too rapidly and would soon interfere with our coast watching activities. I sent a message to Station KEN asking for Sorem Village to be bombed.

Mackenzie arranged for the attack to take place on the night of January 13. The plan called for a team of my boys to make their way under cover of darkness to the outskirts of town where daylight aerial reconnaissance had revealed a certain grass hut near the village. My men were instructed to lie in wait until they heard a plane approaching, then to set fire to the shack as a guide for the aircraft and to run as fast as possible away from the target area. The natives, led by Sergeant Yauwika, showed a lot of courage in volunteering for the mission, and it was executed to perfection.

A Catalina carried out the raid. The pilot made three runs over the village at 1,500 feet, dropping two 500-pound bombs, a cluster of incendiaries, and a couple of depth charges. This probably sounds like a powerful discharge of explosives on a small native settlement, but fortunately only one person was slightly wounded. However, the gesture and resulting shock value served our purpose.

Much to our astonishment, the surprise bombardment even unnerved the enemy. A few days after the attack on Sorem, the Japanese commander at the Passage summoned all the area native chiefs to Sohano where they were addressed by the commandant. He informed the people that U.S. forces were expected to invade northern Bougainville and that his troops might have to retreat for a few days until they could launch a counterattack.

In case of such an eventuality, the natives were ordered to assist and feed the Japanese soldiers. Beach villages were instructed to institute a system of constant vigilance—reporting anything unusual to Sohano immediately. The chieftains were also warned against sending any information to me, and that henceforth the airfield and all fortified positions were off-limits. Finally, the chiefs were advised to protect their people by building air raid shelters.

While the speech did not enhance Japanese prestige in the eyes of the natives, fear of the consequences weighed heavily on the minds of the village leaders. More importantly, however, was the fact that this display of panic on the part of the enemy was the first intimation to the islanders that their conquerors were not the invincible beings they professed to be. The stern lecture and warnings certainly contradicted earlier Japanese assertions that the war was over and they had won it.

Frightened natives, in the vicinity of the Passage, now tended to migrate toward Soraken and away from the threatened danger. For the moment, at least, we were afforded a breathing spell.

Meanwhile, conditions were not going well with Paul Mason. His reappearance on the air was brief. The whole Buin area was overrun with enemy soldiers. Allied bombing and strafing of Kieta villages did not deter the pro-Japanese natives from leading patrols in pursuit of the coast watchers.

About the middle of January, Mackenzie directed Mason to abandon his operation and join me in northern Bougainville. When the enemy net began to draw tight around Porapora, I took the precaution of transferring the bulky teleradio to a secluded location about a mile deeper into the mountains. In order to reach the site it was necessary to wade along a small stream for about a half hour. We left no footprints to be followed. One of my police boys remained at the original vantage point, ready to relay information, by runner, back to the radio station.

Paul Mason linked up with McLean's party at Mainuki and they pushed northward together, eventually arriving at my hideout a fortnight later. The new post was so hard for them to find that Mason and his natives, all expert bushmen, had a difficult time locating my position.

Stores were dropped to us on the night of January 22, and again three nights later. These two drops totaled 4,000 pounds and consisted of 26 parachutes and 40 dumps. Unfortunately, a large portion of this consignment was destroyed when a number of chutes failed to open. Included in these shipments was an undamaged teleradio unit, which was sent for the purpose of equipping a coast watching party to overlook Kieta Harbor.

Early in February, Corporal Dolby, accompanied by Wigley and two other soldiers, headed south to set up this new base. However, the mission was doomed for failure. Their call sign, LBY, was never heard on the air. The team traveled down the coast by canoes and went ashore at the Tenakow Plantation. Unknown to Dolby was the fact that the Japanese had recently established outposts at several points from Kieta north to Tenakow and Numa Numa. The AIF detachment ran into enemy troops and were lucky to get clear of the area. They were forced to abandon everything but the transmitter apparatus. Wigley was cut off from the others and was listed as missing for several days. He finally rejoined his outfit at Namatoa, but fell sick as a result of the hardships he endured while attempting to elude the Nipponese.

Japanese expansion, along the east coast of Bougainville, drove a wedge deep into our vitals. Harry Cameron's post at Inus was betrayed by a Kiviri Village native. Cameron and his handful of men were lucky to escape a surprise raid by an enemy patrol. The Kiviri traitor was later apprehended and executed by a firing squad.

The Chinese community, hidden behind Numa Numa, was routed by the Japs and forced to live a seminomadic, hand-to-mouth existence in the hills. It was an especially pitiful plight for their many young children.

Mack Lee, an Asiatic trader, fell prey to enemy barbarism. Before his death he was tortured. Lee's tongue was cut from his mouth and his eyes were burned out.

We also heard other stories of Japanese brutality. Frank Roche, a gold miner from Atamo, had been murdered. The natives of Vito Village led an enemy patrol inland to Roche's camp. Roche was a hunchback, and, according to reports, the Japs had looped a rope around the poor man's neck and drawn it down between his legs, forcing his head down to the level of his knees. They then forced him to trot along ahead of them, like a large, clumsy dog on a leash. After the hoodlums had hiked with their victim about three miles, they tired of the sport. One of the Japs drew his sword and chopped off Roche's head. The enemy soldiers then sat down to lunch a few feet from the body. Father Muller, who later became a captive, found the miner's remains the next day and gave him a Christian burial.

These same Vito people also had other crimes to answer for. The family of See To Kui had hidden in the hills with other Chinese refugees when the Japanese invaded Kieta. The Orientals scattered when the enemy approached, but the Vito gangsters saw to it that See To Kui's wife and attractive daughter were not captured. When the Japs departed with all the male Chinese that they were able to round up, the natives apprehended the two women and took them to the village square. The women were then tied to posts, publicly stripped, and subjected to an ordeal of indecency until they died.

The people of Roruana Village were just as bad. They betrayed Wong You. He was in hiding with several other Chinese men, women, and children. The Japanese captured the entire group.

Meanwhile, back at my neck of the woods, the natives of Taiof Island jumped into the enemy camp. They captured two of my scouts and delivered them to Sohano. I asked Mackenzie if it was possible to have their village bombed. However, it seemed that other factors now stood in the way of such means of retribution. I was informed that future bombing of native villages could only be carried out with the express approval of Admiral William Halsey—and then only if my safety was at stake. I suspect that this decision was sincere and based on humane grounds of some sort.

However, I hasten to add that there was never any indiscriminate bombing of villages in Bougainville. The few attacks authorized were carried out for specific purposes legitimate to the war effort. The comparatively few anti-European, or pro-Japanese, incidents that occurred are indicative of just what we were up against as regards the situation on the island. As an official of the administration, and protector of the native population, I would be the first to criticize myself to anything of the contrary.

I never requested any further bombings, although the need for them became infinitely greater as time passed. In fact, almost on the eve of our enforced exit from the island, pro-Japanese natives captured five of our exhausted soldiers and airmen and handed them over to the enemy garrison at Numa Numa.

In the early months of 1943, Japanese shipping around the Passage continued busy as ever, unloading cargo after cargo of supplies and equipment. Activity at the Buka airstrip also maintained a nonstop schedule. Bomber formations, flying in from the northwest, continued to draw their fighter escorts from Buka. However, the new airfield at Kahili was becoming more prominent.

On February 10, I received word that American forces had captured Guadalcanal. There was no news that could have been more welcome, for it placed Bougainville just that much closer to liberation. Equally satisfying were the following signals of commendation:

A large share of credit for our successes against the enemy are due to the splendid men in the coast watching service. —Admiral Richmond K. Turner, U.S. Navy.

Your magnificent and courageous work has contributed in great measure to the success of our operations on Guadalcanal.

—General Alexander M. Patch, U.S. Army

The men of the coast watching teams, who had been of the greatest assistance, also came in for their share of official recognition. Mackie, Wigley, Sly, and Otton were each awarded the U.S. Silver Star Medal. Sergeant Yauwika received the Australian Commendation Medal.

It was quickly becoming obvious, for a number of reasons, that our coast watching efforts were not up to previous standards. The efficiency of earlier operations had been made possible by Japanese nonintervention. However, the events of the next few months were to prove the impossibility of maintaining that proficiency.

At this time, BTU was actually the only station on the air, but it only covered northern Bougainville. Japanese expansion in other parts of the island would require additional observation posts. We had the manpower, but not the necessary wireless sets.

Lieutenant Commander Mackenzie proposed to expand the scope of our operations and increase our strength. Captain Eric Robinson and Lieutenant George Stevenson, of the AIF, and Sub-Lieutenant Jack Keenan, of the Royal Australian Navy Volunteer Reserve, were assigned to reinforce our tenuous position on the island. They were ideal men to handle coast watching sites. Each was familiar with the local conditions on Bougainville and each was well known to the natives.

I formulated a scheme, subject to the approval of Mackenzie and the arrival of these officers with teleradio equipment. My plan provided for the reorganization of coast watching on Bougainville.

Briefly, the strategy called for establishing at least four wireless outposts to be located far back in the mountains and covering specified sections of the island. Small mobile patrols, carrying portable radio sets, and venturing close to enemy strong points, would relay messages back to their bases. From there the information could be signaled to Guadalcanal. In theory, this plan would give us complete coverage of Bougainville, and the project was immediately approved by Mackenzie.

With knowledge that a submarine would soon be delivering reinforcements to the island, I began to explore the possibility of evacuating the Chinese women and children who had not yet been captured by the Japanese. I considered myself morally responsible for their predicament. At my instigation, they left Buka Passage to avoid the enemy, and since then they had ignored Japanese enticements to return and reopen their stores. But, because they continued to evade the Nips, the Orientals now feared for their lives.

The Chinese had never been given the opportunities afforded the Europeans. The prejudice of color made it convenient to forget that they were also our allies.

Enemy occupation of Numa Numa rendered the drop site at Inus unsafe. My next choice was a natural clearing behind the Tearouki Plantation. We received two shipments at this location—one on the night of February 25 and another a week later. Aircraft patrols from Buka did not interfere with our supply line.

However, a Japanese detachment of 150 soldiers nearly upset our plans for the first drop at Tearouki. The enemy patrol did not seem to have any specific objective in mind. They moved out from their base at Porton and headed up the trail leading to Porapora. My lookouts immediately packed up and hurried to Lumsis. But, for some unknown reason, when the Japs came to within a mile of Porapora, they turned back and took the path to Baniu Bay. When they reached Baniu, the troops followed the coast road past Raua, Tinputz, and Teop—moving as far south as the Inus Plantation. At that point, they turned around. But, before returning over the same route, the Japs camped at Tearouki and departed the site a day prior to our supply delivery. Natives reported that the enemy soldiers had inquired about the location of the AIF.

Soon after the drop, I was surprised by Lieutenant Mackie's request for me to send a message to Australian Army Headquarters asking for his unit to be relieved. Reluctantly, I sent the following dispatch:

> Mackie to Port Moresby: If enemy occupies Teop, my position on Bougainville will be helpless. Native problems are acute. My movements are now confined to an area from Inus to Raua. If forced to take to the interior, the reception of stores will be impossible. Request immediate evacuation. I accept no responsibility as to the fate of my men if nothing is done. Acknowledge immediately.

I would like to emphasize that our situation was not as precarious as Mackie made it out to be. Therefore, I sent a cover signal to the effect that, under these circumstances, the AIF was of no practical use to me. However, it could be if it were under more experienced leadership. It would be wrong to construe this comment as being derogatory toward Lieutenant Mackie, whom I hold in high esteem. He was, I believe, the youngest member of the Army section, but he was also handicapped by the unique conditions under which he and his men were forced to live.

By now, the Australian soldiers had served continuously for 18 months in the tropics. They were not only jungle-weary, but also susceptible to imaginary grievances—both against their superiors, who they considered had abandoned them, and against each other. Furthermore, they were overly pessimistic regarding the constricting operations of the enemy.

This discontentment could have been largely avoided if the soldiers were permitted to engage in interest-stimulating activities—such as reconnaissance patrols. However, and apparently in accordance with their defensive training, the Army's policy was one of concentration of forces. But, in my opinion, the abnormal conditions prevailing in Bougainville called for modification of normal measures.

Because of this latest hassle, Mackenzie placed Lieutenant Mackie and his men under my command. I did not relish the job. Morale had slipped too far. Lieutenant Commander Feldt must have sensed the problem. He offered to send me a new AIF section to replace Mackie's unit. I accepted the proposal without hesitation—the date of the changeover to be held in abeyance for the time being.

I was also given the option of deciding whether or not I actually wanted an AIF force, but an Army detachment was essential in order to put my plan of intelligence-gathering centers into operation. If I had been able to see a few months ahead, I would have declined the offer. However, better men than I have failed in that respect—and with far greater consequences.

Considering the habits of the Japanese during the past year, it was logical to assume that they would allow us to continue our coast watching work without too much harassment. But enemy expansion was methodically rendering the coastal areas of Bougainville untenable as both base and supply sites. My proposed lookout posts would be located deep into the mountainous interior of the island, making enemy approach extremely difficult. Neither our present base at Namatoa nor the drop site at Tearouki conformed with these new requirements.

I intended to use the experience of Mackie's soldiers to begin making location changes before the new AIF outfit arrived. Reconnaissance revealed a suitable supply site near the village of Dariai, ten miles farther inland from Namatoa. On March 23, we received our first shipment of stores at Dariai.

Meanwhile, specific arrangements were made for the relief mission to be effected in two submarine sorties. On the first strip, 12 AIF personnel would be evacuated and a corresponding number landed under the command of Sub-Lieutenant Jack Keenan. The operation was scheduled for March 28, 1943, at Teop Harbor, with a second trip a month later.

On the evening of the 28th, Teop was still free of enemy troops. Paul Mason was standing by to signal any approach by the Japanese from the direction of Numa Numa. A scouting party, led by Harry Cameron, was stationed to warn of enemy infiltration from the north. Lieutenant Mackie, with the help of Usaia Sotutu and Sergeant Yauwika, made all necessary preparations at the beach.

The proposed outgoing people were in readiness and listed in order of priority in case the ship was unable to accommodate the entire party. Father Lebel was ready to have three more elderly Sisters carried to the beach. McGarrell and Waterhouse were stationed inland to shepherd the Chinese women and children to the harbor.

The evacuation was going along as planned, when suddenly a small Japanese coastal vessel hove into view. Our scouts had been following the craft as it moved south past Tinputz. The vessel turned into Teop Harbor and anchored off the very spot we had chosen for the operation. Warnings were immediately dispatched to all parties to hold everything, and I sent a signal to both stations KEN and VIG. The evacuation was postponed until the following night. My scouts kept the enemy ship under constant surveillance. Five Japs and several Kieta natives were aboard the coastal schooner. It lay idly at anchor until morning and then continued south toward Kieta.

At dusk on the 29th, all evacuees had arrived at the beach and signal fires were lit. Within a few minutes, the U.S.S. *Gato* surfaced in the harbor and moved about a hundred yards from our position on the shore.

I paddled a canoe out to the submarine and talked with the ship's skipper, Lieutenant Commander Robert J. Foley. The captain had been advised that there were 24 people to be evacuated—12 Army personnel and the same number of refugees. I told Foley that the group had grown considerably and now totaled 51 people. The *Gato*'s commander and his navigation officer, Lieutenant Ward, discussed the situation. After a few minutes, they agreed to try and take the entire lot.

This was a speedier rescue than the one on New Year's Eve. A flotilla of canoes, manned by loyal Teop Islanders, plied rapidly between the beach and the sub. In less than an hour, all passengers had been crammed aboard, and the incoming personnel were landed. Shortly after 9 P.M. the ship headed for the open sea.

Included in the evacuation party were Usaia Sotutu's wife and the Sotutus' five children and Mrs. Pitt and her two daughters. I also took advantage of this opportunity to send out the financial and banking records of the Buka Passage and Kieta districts. I had been hauling them around the bush for nearly a year.

Lieutenant Commander Foley related one interesting fact to me. The *Gato* had actually been submerged in Teop Harbor since the previous afternoon, and, during the night, it surfaced quite close to the Japanese vessel. Only the fear of jeopardizing the evacuation prevented the submarine's gun crew from destroying the enemy ship.

The incoming Army detachment was commanded by Jack Keenan and Lieutenant Douglas Bedkober. In addition to new teleradios, the AIF detachment was also supplied with a number of small portable wireless sets known as Type 208. They were designed by the Army for short-distance telegraph communications between mobile patrol parties and their bases. Each unit only weighed nine pounds complete with all accessories. It was mounted in a small metal case and could be conveniently slung in a haversack.

By dawn on March 30, the fresh Army troops and their equipment had reached Namatoa. Nothing remained on the beach to reveal what had occurred the night before. And once again we were in luck. No sooner had we arrived at the AIF base than a schooner and a couple of barges pulled into Teop Harbor. They were en route from Numa Numa to the Buka Passage. The bandits foraged around Tearouki Plantation for a few hours and then continued north.

The arrival of Keenan and his men lifted our morale considerably. In pre-war days, Jack had served extensively as a patrol officer at the Passage and at Kieta. He brought with him two Buka Island natives who had been captured at Rabaul and used as forced laborers at Buna, New Guinea. These natives proved to be of excellent propaganda value to us. They wandered among the local people, telling stories of Japanese defeats at Guadalcanal, Buna, and Milne Bay. This firsthand information seemed more convincing to the villagers when it came from their own kith and kin.

The former prisoners also carried a selection of photographs showing the expanding war industry in Australia. They were accorded an interested audience in every community they visited, and their efforts enabled us to hold the pro-Japanese natives at bay—at least for the time being.

I was impressed with the enthusiasm and ambition of Lieutenant Bedkober and his Army lads. They were eager for the job ahead and anxious to absorb every bit of knowledge available from Mackie's men.

The principal objective of my plan was for each teleradio to be hidden in the mountains, and at the most inaccessible location possible. One or more patrol squads, carrying portable wireless sets, would be attached to each outpost.

In theory, a couple of Type 208's could be able to cover a radius of at least 25 miles. A single coast watching station would employ a half-dozen soldiers, including three expert signalmen, and about a dozen trusted natives. The remote placement of the camps would render them more or less safe from Japanese interference—while the forward patrols, operating close to enemy lines, had the advantage and protection of mobility.

I realized, of course, that my strategy could not be fully implemented until the rest of the incoming Army personnel, under Captain Robinson and Lieutenant Stevenson, arrived on April 28.

I intended to send Paul Mason and George Stevenson south to establish a base overlooking the Kieta-Buin area. Sergeant G. J. McPhee would take up a position covering the midwest coast of the island, and Eric Robinson would join me at Namatoa. I arranged with Jack Keenan to take over my Buka Passage base while I searched the mountains for a central location to cover the east coast of Bougainville.

Keenan set up his camp at Lumsis, with a forward lookout post at Porapora. Under the call sign PLG he was soon reporting information directly to KEN.

I planned for each coast watching party to be equipped with a teleradio and at least one portable unit. Signalmen would be appropriated from Lieutenant Bedkober's outfit. With the balance of his men, Bedkober would establish additional bases wherever necessary. This group would also be available to prepare drop sites, arrange for the receipt and dispersal of stores, and other matters in conjunction with the maintenance of the coast watching posts.

During the next few weeks, Lieutenant Bedkober organized a series of short reconnaissance patrols to test the midget radio sets under various conditions and distances. One of his portable transmitters sent a message 50 miles. This experiment occurred at midday and with high, intervening mountains. The test fulfilled all of our requirements, and I could visualize excellent results from their operation.

We only experienced one fault with the Type 208: the metal casing was not insulated against humidity. Sweating was so profuse that it often caused short circuits in the wireless set. Whenever this happened, it became necessary to dry out the complete unit over a fire.

There were several facts about working in enemy territory that I tried to impress on the new arrivals. Careless coding of signals can easily detract from otherwise good coast watching efforts. Rarely is a signal of such extreme urgency that a few minutes cannot be devoted to checking the code before sending the dispatch. Transmissions should be cut to a minimum and only when the message is essential. Calls should be short because the enemy is probably listening to our signals and probably trying to copy down everything said. It must be remembered that the Japanese have decoding experts the same as we have.

Mason, meanwhile, remained at Numa Numa, overlooking enemy activity and signaled under the call sign NDT. I continued to work from Namatoa in order to keep a close watch on Teop Harbor.

Having already pressed my luck by carrying out two evacuations under the very eyes of the Japanese, Mackenzie ques-

tioned the wisdom of again using the site. However, Teop possessed all the facilities we needed to carry out this kind of operation. We had canoes, paddlers, and trusted native carriers
right on the spot, and it provided a quick getaway to the interior. I did not wish to abandon the location for another unless
I was forced to do so by enemy intervention. The expert manner with which Lieutenant Commander Foley brought his ship
into the harbor proved that nothing short of Japanese occupation of Teop could interfere with our plans—provided, of
course, that future evacuations were carried out on the same
basis and according to a strict schedule.

In view of the large number of evacuees I had been able to
send out on the previous trip, I felt confident of being able to
ship out the remaining male civilians, missionaries, and Asiatics
on the forthcoming trip. They were all conveniently located,
with the exception of Bishop Wade, who was hiding somewhere in the mountains between Kieta and Puruata. I knew
that Wade would never leave his diocese unless ordered to do
so by a superior. I discussed the matter with Father Lebel, the
outcome being that he undertook the long trek through the
interior in quest of his bishop.

Lebel returned with Bishop Wade a few days before the
end of the month. The last meeting I had with Wade occurred
near Tinputz the day after Kieta had been allegedly occupied
by the Japanese. He was now a broken man, mentally and phys-
ically, and he had no choice but to agree to my demand that
he should be evacuated.

In the meantime, enemy forces continued to expand their
stranglehold on the northern Solomons. Buka Island was hon-
eycombed with outposts, and Matchin Bay had been settled
from the Passage as far south as Porton. Japanese troops regularly patrolled the east coast from the Passage to Baniu Bay.

Aerial activity also began to increase as fighter formations
were observed heading southeast. The heaviest flight was
sighted on April 7, when a formation of 48 Zeros were spotted.
Ten minutes later, 50 more fighters were reported on the same

course. All of these aircraft took off from Buka—a good indication of the growth of that airstrip.

I believe, that on this particular day, our warnings enabled American planes to intercept the Japs before they reached their target. Heavy casualties were inflicted on the enemy squadrons.

Early in the month, enemy survey teams began scouting the east coast of Bougainville for possible airfield locations. The Inus Plantation, Numa Numa, and Tenakow were thoroughly investigated.

Tinputz was formally occupied by the Japanese on April 14, and another detachment searched Teopasina for a few days and then withdrew. Small coastal steamers moved constantly up and down the eastern shore, and there were grandiose rumors that the Japs planned to construct an elegant highway from the Buka Passage to Kieta.

Paul Mason reported a large influx of enemy troops in the Numa Numa and Tenakow vicinity. Evidently these soldiers comprised men who had recently been evacuated from Guadalcanal. They were emaciated, barefoot, and clad only in rags. Most of them were without weapons. Other Japanese would point out these hapless humans to the natives as being in disgrace because of their humiliating defeat.

Our most immediate concern, however, was the enemy occupation of Tinputz. It was uncomfortably close to our evacuation site at Teop Harbor. The Japs landed an advance force of about a hundred men and immediately sent out small, six- to eight-man parties, to penetrate various trails into the foothills.

My police boys continually returned with reports of these scouting movements and requested permission to ambush the enemy patrols. But, for fear of jeopardizing the approaching second trip of the submarine, I could not sanction such action.

The temptation proved too much for Corporal Sanei. His job was to watch the path about a mile below my camp. On April 16, a half-dozen Japanese approached his position. Sanei alleged that he was fired upon first, but I will always suspect the truth of that statement. At any rate, the police boy, armed with a rifle that had a defective bolt, fired on the Japs and scattered the patrol. He dropped three of the soldiers, whereupon the others picked up their wounded comrades and escaped toward Tinputz. Two of the men later died and were cremated on the beach.

Humbly and apologetically, Corporal Sanei duly reported his "trophies" of the hunt—equipment hurriedly discarded by the Japanese in their flight. Although he had disobeyed orders, I must confess that I admired the loyalty and courage of this Redskin in his lone venture. It was typical of the spirit of these lads whom I had been able to hold in my service for so long a period. Sanei proudly stated that if his old rifle had not been defective he would have killed the whole lot.

For my part, however, I began to speculate on possible enemy reaction to the attack—but nothing happened. In many respects it seemed to take the Nips a long time to wake up. To be on the safe side, I notified Mackenzie to change the evacuation site to the beach at Teopasina, a few miles farther down the coast from Teop. This alternate location would permit a longer warning in the event more Japanese patrols scouted south from Tinputz. The area also afforded all the facilities of Teop.

About this time, the mountainous Aita region, a full day's journey from Dariai, came under consideration as an additional drop site. The distinct possibility of further enemy encroachment would necessitate the moving of our supplies from one base to another. To avoid the arduous task of shifting stores, I planned to let the Catalinas do the job for us. We would set up a succession of bases and sites for various supply missions. Dariai was the first link in the chain, and it had been well stocked by the previous month's air drop. Aita was selected as the next link. Corporal Bill Dolby led a squad into the area to prepare a site for the subsequent supply shipment. He was provided with a teleradio to keep me informed of his movements.

At noon, on April 21, Lieutenant Commander Pryce-Jones replaced Hugh Mackenzie at Guadalcanal Headquarters.

Mackenzie was transferred to Brisbane due to the ill health of Eric Feldt. I was upset by the fact that we were losing direct touch with a man who spoke our language, knew our problems, and had been able to tide us over many difficult times on Bougainville.

Meanwhile, Corporal Dolby had progressed rapidly with his job at Aita. Full particulars of the new site were signaled to Australia, and a supply mission was scheduled for the night of April 26. In absence of information to the contrary, I assumed that the usual aerial reconnaissance of the location had been made beforehand. Unfortunately, however, this was not the case.

Early the next morning, Dolby reported that the first of two Catalinas assigned to the task had crashed in the nearby mountains while making its second run over the drop zone. Three members of the crew were killed outright and six injured airmen were rescued.

I pieced together the story of the accident from the accounts related by the survivors. Sergeant F. G. Thompson, of the Royal Australian Airforce, reported his version of the air crash:

> At 1500 hours, our Catalina, captained by Flight Lieutenant W. J. Clark, took off from Cairns, Australia to drop supplies at Aita, Bougainville.
>
> The Aita site was located at 2300 hours without difficulty, at which time we were flying at 10,000 feet. The sky was clear but the moon had not yet risen.
>
> Before commencing the drop, Corporal H. Yates removed the port gun and stowed it on the starboard side of the blister. We then began unloading packages. After a couple of circuits of the area, and dropping two parachutes, the captain asked over the intercom if the third chute was ready. Pilot Officer C. J. Twist replied in the negative. Flight Lieutenant Clark then started to make a right-hand turn. Moments later we felt a jolt and heard the engines rev at full power. The time was approximately 2330.

Thompson did not remember any other details. However, Corporal R. N. Wettenhall recalled the aircraft hitting trees followed by violent bumps. Then all was quiet except for the dripping of leaking fuel. There was complete darkness.

Corporals Yates and Wettenhall called out to ascertain the condition of the rest of the crew, but there was no reply. Wettenhall managed to free himself from the wreckage and struggled aft. Yates suddenly heard Thompson cry out for help and stumbled forward to free Thompson from the crushed plane. Flight Officer C. S. Dunn, smelling the leaking gasoline, somehow was able to crawl out of the crushed Catalina. The men were unable to find a flashlight, and it was too dangerous to use matches, so they decided to remain with the plane until dawn. During the night the other Catalina was seen and heard as it passed over the drop zone in the moonlight.

At daybreak, Corporal Wettenhall, using a gun cleaning rod, smashed the starboard blister to remove the wounded. The noise attracted Dolby's AIF party who had been hunting all night for the downed aircraft.

Sergeant H. Broadfoot was one of the first soldiers to reach the scene of the disaster. He fired his pistol as a signal to the other searchers that he had found the plane. Sergeant Walter Radimey and his men quickly arrived with first-aid supplies.

Flight Lieutenant Clark, Flight Officer J. N. Potts, and Sergeant D. J. Ward were found to have been killed instantly in the crash. The rescue team removed a couple of bunks from the Catalina to use as stretchers, and natives made additional litters to carry the injured. Most of the stores were salvaged from the wreck. Dolby and his detachment carried the wounded and the supplies back to the Aita drop zone.

I thought it would be possible to transport the airmen down to the beach at Teopasina by dusk on April 29, and I received permission to postpone the evacuation for 24 hours. I wanted to get the air crash survivors off our hands immediately, but fate decreed otherwise. The injured would have had to be carried across very rugged terrain. Nevertheless, they still could have made it through if it were not for heavy rains and flooded rivers. Because of the uncertainty of our position, I did not feel justified in asking for another postponement of the evacuation. It was just another case of bad luck.

While the more seriously injured were being tended to at Aita by Sergeant Radimey, Corporal Yates and Pilot Officer Twist walked back to the scene of the accident. They had climbed about 300 yards up a hill when they came to a ridge with a sheer drop into the valley below. Yates noticed that the tops of tall trees in front of the cliff had been clipped off, and directly below the bluff was the starboard wing of the Catalina.

Looking down from the ridge, the narrow, slicing trail of the crashing aircraft could be seen as it smashed through trees and underbrush. About 300 yards down the cliff, the Catalina was spotted lying on its starboard side. The port wing and center section were parallel to the ground. The front of the plane, as far aft as the engineer's compartment, was crushed beyond recognition.

A few hours later, an AIF party tried unsuccessfully to recover the bodies from the aircraft. They destroyed anything that could prove of value to the enemy and then camouflaged the Catalina with trees and brush.

Early on the morning of the 29th, Dolby and his men headed back to Dariai with the recovered supplies. Pilot Officer Twist and Corporal Yates were able to walk to the base, while Sergeant Thompson and Corporal Wettenhall were carried on stretchers. Because of a shortage of natives, Flight Officer Dunn and Corporal J. Fenwick spent a day and a night at Aita. Sergeant Radimey remained with the two injured airmen until the litter bearers returned. They reached Dariai on April 30.

In the meantime, I was going ahead with our evacuation plans. The nearest points of Japanese occupation were about six miles above Teopasina and at Numa Numa, 30 miles farther down the coast. Sergeants B. Cohen, J. Collier, and W. Florance were stationed at a forward position to give immediate warning of any enemy movement from Tinputz. Sergeants McPhee and F. Furner were posted near the Inus Plantation and covered the Numa Numa region. Paul Mason and Jack Keenan were charged with the management of everything at the evacuation site.

Accompanied by Signalman A. Falls, I set up my teleradio at a central location overlooking the coastline of the entire area. The outposts were equipped with portable radios, and each station was under orders to maintain a constant listening watch on a prearranged common frequency. Using this system, an alarm signal from any mobile unit would be immediately picked up by all bases, and acted upon according to my instructions. If the need arose, I was in a position to communicate instantly either with VIG or KEN about the operation. It was an ideal network to guard against enemy intrusion on the rescue area.

The evacuees were already making their way from various parts of the mountains to the departure site. Everyone timed their arrival to be at Teopasina at dusk on the 29th. The group scheduled to leave on the submarine totaled 23 people. The list included Lieutenant Mackie and the balance of his AIF unit, Bishop Wade along with the rest of the missionaries still on the island, and Bob Stuart.

I held up on evacuating the Chinese, hoping that the Catalina crew might be able to reach the site in time. But it was too late to change the plan, and the Asiatics were camped another day's journey inland.

The Teop Islanders and their canoes reached Teopasina about dark. Signal fires were lighted, but were hard to keep burning because of frequent rain squalls. Time passed slowly for the men huddled in the rain on the beach. They strained their eyes seaward, searching the water for a glimpse of the ship.

Finally, about 11 P.M., the *Gato* was sighted. Lieutenant Commander Foley expertly maneuvered his submarine through the reef-ridden harbor to within hailing distance of the beach. Once again, the natives paddled their canoes back and forth— carrying the evacuees out to the ship, and returning with the incoming personnel along with stores and equipment.

Several minutes later, the *Gato* put back to sea. The retiring signal was flashed to the outposts and acknowledged. Mason directed Captain Robinson and Lieutenant Stevenson to my camp, while Keenan and the new AIF soldiers headed for Dariai.

CHAPTER 10

Heading North

JANUARY 2–APRIL 30, 1943

Paul Mason

The first two weeks of 1943, we remained at Siuru. No supplies had been dropped to us for a month. My party was still on the run, and I had been off the air for more than a fortnight. When I finally made contact with Station KEN, I was instructed to close my outpost, abandon the wireless, and head north to join Jack Read. I removed the most valuable parts of the teleradio and hid them in the scrub, leaving the rest of the equipment in a vacant native hut.

Accompanied by Wigley, Otton, and four police boys, I proceeded west through the Siwai District. As we sneaked quietly along the jungle trails, native villagers could be heard beating on their wooden drums—warning the people that Japanese patrols were advancing into the area.

That same night, we forded the Puriata River and crossed into the "badlands" of Negavisi. Japanese propaganda had done its work well in this vicinity. With the help of Kieta natives, the enemy had turned the local natives into treacherous servants of the Emperor. We slept in the bush above Soveli, and the following day we reached Konkapina near the Jaba River.

While at the village, I met Father Grisward, who was also fleeing from the enemy. He informed me that the Japanese were positioned all along the west coast and planned to intercept us at Puruata. I had no choice but to reverse our course and head northeast.

After another day's grueling march, we arrived at Mainuki. It was here that I learned the facts concerning Corporal McLean and his Army unit, who had been sent to search for us. They waited at the village for six days and left for Negavisi only a few hours before we showed up. I immediately sent a runner to locate McLean and tell him that we were at Mainuki.

While waiting for the AIF detachment to return, I decided to set out by myself to Wong You's hideout at Korpe. I was curious as to conditions at Kieta and to know if it was safe to proceed north using the coastal trail. I wished to travel light, so I left my pack and rifle with Wigley and Otton. I ordered them to wait for me until noon of the following day, when I would either return or forward further instructions.

After a five-hour trek, I reached Wong You's camp. It was already 10 P.M., and we talked for about two hours. I borrowed a couple of blankets, and told Wong You where I would be sleeping in the bush nearby. I was awakened two hours later and informed that a Japanese patrol was on its way from Roruana to Korpe. Although I wanted to stay and see what the enemy was up to, I was anxious about McLean's party. I expected them to be back at Mainuki by midday.

In order not to betray Wong You and the rest of the refugee Chinese community, I entered and left the camp barefooted to avoid being tracked. However, in the darkness, I tore the instep of my left foot on lawyer vine.

At daylight, I discovered that I had overshot Mainuki and sent a message to Wigley by a friendly native. But when the lad reached the village, he was told that McLean had arrived the night before. For some unknown reason, Corporal McLean decided not to wait for me to return. He led his outfit north along the Korpe-Atamo trail. Wigley and Otton went with him, expecting to meet me along the road. When they neared Korpe, natives informed the Army group that the Japs had raided the Chinese camp and captured Wong You. The AIF detachment then headed directly to Atamo.

After I received this information from my runner, I put my boots back on and hobbled, as best I could, along the path north toward Atamo. Because of the throbbing pain in my foot, I soon realized that I would be unable to catch up with the soldiers. I dispatched another native runner, by the name of Constable Kiabi, to find the Army boys and tell them of my predicament.

By dusk, I was very tired and hungry. I had had only an hour's sleep the night before. My foot had become infected, but I was afraid to take off the boot. I covered myself with banana leaves and slept soundly in spite of the damp cold. I reached Atamo the following afternoon. Kiabi greeted me at the village. I learned that he had caught up with the soldiers the day before. Otton gave Kiabi my pack and rifle and told the native to take them back along the trail to me. However, afraid of not finding me, Kiabi decided to wait at Atamo until I arrived.

During the night, McLean and his party had left the village. He ordered Wigley, Otton, and my police boys to go with him. They also confiscated my supplies. In my opinion, the conduct of Corporal McLean and his men amounted to desertion. And I was not about to forget their abandoning me. Since I was a naval officer, our relationship, as to who was in charge, had never been properly settled.

While I rested at Atamo, I located Frank Roche hiding in the bush. At one time, Roche worked for me at the Inus Plantation. When the war began, he was operating a gold mine claim. I decided to stay with Frank for a while and treat my foot. When I removed the left boot, for the first time in 36 hours, the sock and septic flesh from the instep came off with it. I doctored the foot for two days. The wound was still sore, but I had to get moving. I bandaged the leg and pushed on, barefooted, accompanied by Kiabi.

We traveled north, keeping well inland at first, then striking the coast near the Kurwina Plantation. I was in great pain and could hardly walk, but with Kiabi's help I managed to reach Asitave. The short journey took us three days. I was welcomed at the village by Fathers O'Sullivan and Fluet. Brothers Paul, Jules, and Henry were also camped at the refuge, along with two elderly Sisters, one of whom was a cripple. Father O'Sullivan had rescued the women from the Buin and Siwai districts.

After giving my foot a day to heal, I continued north to Inus, stopping at Kubum, adjacent to the plantation. As soon as the natives, many of whom I knew very well, learned of my arrival, I was given the friendliest welcome since I escaped from the Buin area. I was not permitted to walk, but was carried, with much ceremony, to a waiting canoe. A flotilla of well-wishers, paddling outriggers, followed us along the coast to Teop Harbor. From there, we took the trail to the AIF camp at Namatoa.

I was greeted by Lieutenant Mackie and his lads, but I was in no mood for compliments or congratulations. I immediately jumped all over McLean for clearing out of Atamo without waiting for me. But that was not the only thing that irritated me about this Army gang. I was astonished at the comfortable living quarters that the AIF had set up for themselves. They had scrounged furniture and equipment from vacated plantations. I even recognized some of my own property stolen from Inus. More unbelievable, however, was the fact that, in their huts, the soldiers had installed kerosene mantle lamps that burned brightly every night.

The next day, in company with Kiabi and a few police boys, I headed for Porapora. We climbed the mountainous terrain for two days, finally arriving at Jack Read's camp on January 28. I had not seen Read for 12 months and was delighted to meet him again. I remained at the outpost for a fortnight while my foot healed. While at Porapora, I got to know Jack personally and acquired a good working knowledge of his methods.

As Japanese patrols started to become more aggressive, we were forced to abandon the forward position, and so we reestablished our location at Lumsis. We had no sooner set up the teleradio than Lieutenant Mackie asked for his AIF unit to be relieved. Jack and I both thought that some of the older, and more hard-boiled, soldiers instigated the action.

On one occasion, while Read was away, I received a message from Mackenzie asking what we both felt about the Army detachment. I relayed the signal to Jack, but also sent a reply of my own. I stated that I believed Read would endorse my judgment that the soldiers in Bougainville were useless. Much to my surprise, when Jack returned, he dispatched a message to KEN disagreeing with my opinion. Evidently, he hoped to make competent soldiers out of the men.

Read was placed in charge of the Army troops and also became my senior officer. I was sent to establish a coast watching post at Yauwun Village, a short distance above the Inus Plantation. I operated under the call sign NDT. There was little to be observed apart from the movements of Japanese barges and patrols. However, a submarine was expected to arrive near the end of March, and my main job was to watch the coast as a precautionary measure.

The ship arrived on the night of March 29 and evacuated half the AIF detachment. Sub-Lieutenant Jack Keenan and a new group of soldiers, under Lieutenant Bedkober, were landed. I met Keenan the next day and then returned to my post.

Throughout the following month, I reported a great deal of enemy activity at Tenakow and Numa Numa. Read was suffering from a boil on his leg and I was delegated to meet the submarine on its return trip. While waiting for the sub to arrive, we received word that a Catalina had crashed at Aita. All necessary action was taken to rescue the survivors.

The April evacuation went off as scheduled. Captain Robinson and Lieutenant Stevenson came ashore with additional troops, and the balance of Mackie's detachment embarked on the U.S.S. *Gato*. The next day, April 30, Robinson, Stevenson, and I joined Read at Namatoa.

A COMMENT BY DOUGLAS OTTON

Douglas Otton has provided another version of the journey to Wong You's hideout:

Paul Mason's report of what happened when he left us and took off by himself to visit Wong You is very different from what

I and the other soldiers involved experienced. We were on the run at the time, and, under these conditions, the journey to Wong You's hideout was foolhardy and hazardous. Besides, Paul did not gain any information of value. We tried to persuade him not to attempt the trip, as he placed the rest of our group in great danger. In fact, while Mason was away, we heard that he had been captured—and he nearly was.

I was not aware until recently that he blamed us. Paul claimed that I gave his weapon and food to a native. However, as you know, Mason never carried a gun—which was always available to him.

Wigley did practically all the signaling, while I looked after the natives, arranged the drop sites, and shared the watch with Paul. I feel that Mason gave Wigley and myself very little credit for our contribution to that wonderful organization [coast watchers] which did so much to save Guadalcanal. Without our efforts, it might have been a different story.

A COMMENT BY JACK READ

Concerning the conflict between Jack Read and Paul Mason regarding Lieutenant Mackie and his Army unit, Read noted:

Mason's report does not speak too highly of the AIF unit that we had in Bougainville. I also think the men were lacking in some respects. However, it must be remembered that the capacity to endure the sort of existence under which we were forced to live can only be acquired by many years of experience in the tropics. People unaccustomed to this kind of life become somewhat awed with the jungle. In my opinion, therein lies the reason for the tendency to panic on certain occasions. This failing could be overcome by a course in jungle survival procedure.

CHAPTER 11

The Japanese Attack on Porapora and Other Coast Watcher Locations

MAY 1–JULY 19, 1943

Jack Read

As we entered the month of May 1943, the fulfillment of my ambition was in sight. I refer to my coast watching plan to cover enemy activity throughout the island of Bougainville.

Lieutenant Bedkober's men seemed to be just the right sort of new blood we needed, while the older hands were a steady influence. All of us believed that we were aiming for a worthy goal and were imbued with the immense possibilities of the strategy. But perhaps the Japanese did also, for they finally began to demonstrate their irritation of the enemy within their walls.

For the moment, however, the injured airmen were our greatest concern. Whatever comforts we were able to give them could never repay our debt to the men who flew in our supplies on the Catalinas. Several of them, being more or less stretcher cases, would be endangered in the event of an enemy surprise attack. Therefore, our immediate desire was to have them rescued from Bougainville if at all possible.

The Catalina survivors had reached Dariai, and the injured were under the care of Sergeant Walter Radimey. Broken limbs and internal injuries indicated a slow recovery for a few members of the air crew. I signaled for medical supplies, and a successful drop of first-aid items was made on the night of May 10.

My original idea was to have the Catalina boys picked up by a flying boat somewhere between Teop and Inus, but the Japanese occupied the area before the evacuation could be arranged. The only feasible exit from the island now lay on the west coast, but that was a long, difficult journey, and the injured were not in a fit state to be moved. For the moment, it was more convenient for them to recuperate at Dariai, which was about as safe as anywhere else on the island.

Meanwhile, my plan of action began to take shape. Sub-Lieutenant Jack Keenan returned to the Passage area with Sergeant Florance and Corporals A. Little and N. McLeod. They were accompanied by Anton Jossten and Corporal Sali. Florance and McLeod set up a portable radio outpost at Porapora. Keenan and Little established their teleradio base at Lumsis and operated under the call sign PLG.

Paul Mason and Lieutenant George Stevenson organized their party and headed south. They intended to travel from Dariai to Aita and then across to the west coast. Mason's group carried one teleradio and three midget pack sets. Moving lightly and rapidly, their main objective was to push as far south as possible by the full moon and retrieve a supply drop. This would eliminate hauling stores from Dariai.

Using the call sign NDT, Paul would keep in touch with KEN. Subsequent movements of his party would depend on conditions as he penetrated farther into unknown territory. Ever since Mason had been chased out of Buin four months ago, the extent of Japanese occupation in the area had been impossible to determine. The job that lay ahead was going to be tough and dangerous. For this reason, I assigned Usaia Sotutu and eight soldiers to the NDT group.

Paul was averse to taking any Army personnel with him, and it was only at my insistence that he agreed. There was no way that he and Stevenson, by themselves, could have covered more than a small sector of the allocated area. Using the portable radio sets would enable three patrols to work simultaneously and function close to Japanese bases from Kieta to Empress Augusta Bay.

Unfortunately, my strategy was never fully realized. But, if it had been, I feel certain that Mason would have needed every person of his ten-man group and that an excellent job would have been accomplished as a result.

In his statement on the events that transpired [see Chapter 12] Paul remarked that the soldiers did not perform up to his expectations, and there was also the inference that the best personnel were not selected for his expedition. Regarding the former statement, although Paul Mason's opinion is to be respected, I would like to point out the possibility of his standards being somewhat high in conformity with his method of operation. As to the latter, if it exists, I can only state that Lieutenant Bedkober was asked to assign the cream of his men to Mason, and I was not on hand when the selection was made.

Another step toward the objective of my scheme was the establishment of Station GIN in the hinterlands of the midwest coast. There had been practically no enemy ground activity in the area to date. However, I suspected that formations of Japanese aircraft might be flying over the sector en route to Guadalcanal. Sergeant McPhee and Sapper R. Cassidy were placed in charge of the post for the specific purpose of reporting any such flights to KEN.

As for myself, I intended to take up a central position somewhere forward of Aita, overlooking Numa Numa and the east coast of Bougainville. Lieutenant Bedkober had previously detailed a detachment to locate a suitable site where I could move when required. In the meantime, however, I remained at Namatoa covering the recently occupied enemy territory from Tinputz to Teopasina. Captain Robinson and Signalman Alan Falls were with me operating our station under the call sign BTU.

Scouting reports revealed that Japanese strongholds had been established at both Baniu and Raua bays. In my immediate vicinity, the Tinputz garrison was reinforced by several hundred men, and outposts of varying strengths had sprung up at

Tearouki, Teop, and Teopasina. Antiaircraft guns were installed, and emplacements were under construction for large coastal defense guns. From all indications, it began to look as if the enemy was intent on closing all harbors and other points of possible access for Allied amphibious landings.

Expansion of Japanese authority, and the punishment inflicted on pro-British villages, were testing our few loyal districts to the limit. The trend of native feeling was all important to us. Unless we could hold these communities, our future in Bougainville would be short-lived, and that threat now loomed larger than ever.

Mason and his party were already feeling the pinch as they edged toward Empress Augusta Bay, now a veritable hotbed of native sympathy for the Japanese cause. Pressure was also being applied to the Aravia and Lumsis people, who provided sanctuary for Keenan's group. The enemy began to comb the settlements along the coast from Baniu Bay to Numa Numa. Wherever they found a deserted village, the Japs promptly looted and set fire to every house and destroyed the gardens. Not a very encouraging reward for native loyalty or for adherence to my advice for them to steer clear of the enemy. I could only offer abstract promises in return.

When the Japanese set up a permanent garrison at Teop, the Teop Islanders escaped and settled near me at Namatoa. At night, the younger men of the tribe would sneak down to their gardens and bring food back to the women and children. However, these beach people could not withstand the severe climate of the higher elevations and, within a week, several of them had died. Their one-eyed chieftain brought a delegation of elders to our camp. The natives urged that the Americans hurry up to Bougainville before more of their people died. Realizing that the mountains would take a still heavier toll if they remained, I told them to return to their village and outwardly give themselves up to the Japanese, but inwardly stay loyal to us, which they did. I cannot easily forget the Teop Islanders and the significant service they rendered us in helping with the evacuations.

The best way to win a native over to your side is to treat his ills and, so far as our limited means would permit, we were able to show a little tangible appreciation in that respect to some of the friendly communities. Captain Robinson dispensed medicines and administered hundreds of injections until our stock ran out.

Because of continued enemy pressure, Namatoa was becoming increasingly unsafe. Therefore, on May 19, I moved with Station BTU to Dariai. Namatoa became an outpost in charge of Sergeant Bill Cohen. Carrying one Type 208 set, Cohen's detachment was to maintain regular radio schedules with BTU and report any Japanese activity in their sector.

The following night, two Catalinas made a supply run consisting of 12 parachutes and 25 dumps. These dumps had become the bane of our lives as they hurtled down from the sky and buried themselves in the ground. Serious injuries, possibly fatal, would have resulted if anyone was struck by one of these missiles. In fact, I heard that people had been killed by this manner in parts of New Guinea. It is impossible for men to see the packages falling. I recommended to Station KEN that, if chutes were not available, all dumps should be conspicuously marked in some way.

After observing the drop at Dariai, I decided to discontinue using the site to receive stores. The location was uncomfortably close to the enemy-occupied Tinputz-Teop area, over which the aircraft had to maneuver in order to make their runs over the drop zone. The Japanese would have had to be very dense not to guess what went on that night in the mountains behind them. Aita was also no longer safe following the Catalina crash, but I hoped to have another supply base ready at the next full moon.

By this time, Sergeant Radimey's patients were making good recovery at Dariai. Flight Officer Dunn and Corporal Fenwick, both with broken limbs, were the only men likely to prove cumbersome in case the enemy raided the camp. However, that contingency was being safeguarded to the maximum. In addition to the Catalina crew, seven Chinese men were under our protection at Dariai. They were the last of their colony still free on the island. Most of their wives and children had already been evacuated.

On May 25, I reestablished my teleradio post at a forward position in the Aita vicinity. The new location afforded an excellent panorama of the east coast of Bougainville, including Kieta, Numa Numa, and Tenakow. Below the rocky cliff site, a sheer drop of 2,000 feet ended in the Aita River. The AIF base, adjacent to the tragic crash area, was situated up the valley about five miles to the rear.

I discussed our future plans with Lieutenant Bedkober. It was decided that his extra men would concentrate on two urgent matters: first, moving the surviving airmen from Dariai to the Aita military camp, and then to some point nearer the west coast where they could be rescued by flying boat or submarine; second, scouting the countryside around Aita to find a favorable spot for the next supply delivery.

I actually thought we were on the way to achieving complete success with our coast watching network. But the closest we ever came to full operation of all stations was for a brief period on May 26, 1943. I realized that some day the axe would fall, but I never expected it would drop so soon.

The first blow was struck on the morning of the 26th at Porapora. The camp was betrayed by disloyal natives, and the Japanese launched a surprise raid on the outpost. They rammed home another spike the very next day by attacking Keenan's base at Lumsis. Forewarned by trusted natives, Jack was able to escape with the teleradio, but all stores and personal gear were lost when the enemy completely destroyed the camp. Before closing down his wireless, Keenan notified Guadalcanal that he was going off the air and withdrew a few miles into the bush.

In the report of the assaults on his positions, Sub-Lieutenant Keenan wrote:

On May 25, 1943, I learned that a Japanese patrol, heading inland from Baniu, intended to search the area for our locations. Early the next morning, on our regular scheduled broadcast, I warned Florance and McLeod to be on the alert. They received my signal, but before they could decode the message, a native rushed past their but screaming, "The Japs are here!" McLeod grabbed his rifle. From the doorway he saw several enemy soldiers stealthily approaching at about ten yards. McLeod fired one shot, then dashed to the edge of the nearby cliff. He slid down through the brush, losing his rifle and pistol in the plunge.

Sergeant Florance smashed the wireless on the floor, seized his tommy gun, and raced for the edge of the bluff. He jumped over the side and rolled downhill, losing not only his revolver but also his unlaced boots. Florance lay hidden in the scrub throughout the day about 200 yards from the campsite. The Japs made no attempt to follow them down the slope. The enemy looted the camp and tossed a few grenades in their direction. At nightfall, Florance headed south, eventually joining up with me on May 29. His body had been tom by vines and he was suffering from badly cut feet.

Meanwhile, for the next five days, McLeod sneaked through the jungle, up and down mountains and along creek beds, at all times keeping away from the main trails. He had no food or bedding and covered himself at night with banana leaves. Most of the time he did not wear his boots for fear of leaving shoeprints that could be tracked by the Japanese and their native followers. On the sixth day, he was found by a police boy and brought to my camp. McLeod was in poor physical condition and hurting from numerous wounds on his body, legs, and feet.

I later learned that the enemy patrol was led to Porapora and Lumsis by the Tetakots people, a small community inland from the Baniu Plantation. The most prominent member of the traitors was the native medical official of the village.

Simultaneously with the raid on Porapora, we received word that a Japanese detachment from Tinputz was on its way to Namatoa. I ordered Sergeant Cohen's unit to drop back to Dariai and to move the injured Catalina men and the Chinese to our new base at Aita.

On my direct front, at Numa Numa, no action had yet been taken against us. However, threats continued to run rampant. The coincidence of enemy activity and increasing native support for the Japanese was beginning to loosen the grip that I had maintained for so long on the island.

Whetted by their successes at Porapora and Lumsis, the Japs were now ready to come after us with a vengeance. In a final effort to alienate the natives from the Nipponese, I urged widespread bombing and strafing of enemy-occupied coastal areas from Baniu Bay to Tenakow. The request was immediately complied with.

The first Allied raid was carried out at dusk on May 31, and for several successive nights thereafter. The attack on Numa Numa was the only one that I actually witnessed. The large warehouse on the wharf received a direct hit and exploded in flames. Another bomb fell in the center of troop barracks, and the entire vicinity was subjected to low-altitude strafing. Casualties, among both the Japanese and the natives, were known to be high. Many buildings were gutted by fire, several gun positions were destroyed, and a number of schooners and barges were sunk.

These devastating air raids had the immediate effect of causing the villagers to shun the enemy—but not for long. The Nips were well aware that we were responsible for the sudden attacks on their positions, and they soon redoubled their efforts to put us out of business.

In the meantime, a lack of native carriers was creating a vital holdup in the transporting of people, supplies, and equipment from Dariai to Aita.

Local natives, who were our mainstay in this respect, had deserted following Japanese threats of retribution. This adverse turn of events necessitated a constant alert at Dariai, and it was certainly no place for the helpless airmen. Leaving Captain Robinson in charge at Aita, I left for Dariai on June 4 to speed up evacuation of the base.

It was a full day's journey from my camp to Dariai. En route, I met a stretcher party carrying Flight Officer Dunn to Aita. He appeared to be in good shape but was still a cripple pending the healing of torn thigh muscles. Typical of his indomitable spirit, he lay on the litter with a revolver in one hand and a grenade in the other. I never saw Dunn again. I believe that was the way he eventually went out—taking a bunch of Japs with him. [Actually, Dunn was killed in the Japanese attack on Sikoriapaia.]

I saw Sergeant Florance when I reached Dariai. A team of natives had carried him across country from Keenan's camp. He was still suffering from nasty cuts on his feet and legs received during his pell-mell escape from Porapora. But it would take more than that to subdue this youngster, who had reason to believe that his father was among those allegedly massacred by the Japanese after the fall of Rabaul.

Namatoa was now under enemy occupation, and the threat to Dariai was imminent. There was no alternative but to completely abandon the base and cache the remaining stores and equipment. I hoped to retrieve the supplies at a later date. I made sure the site was completely destroyed before returning to Aita. Within two days a Jap force stormed the camp but found nothing.

I rejoined Captain Robinson and Signalman Falls on June 8. On two occasions, during my absence, Station BTU had been instrumental in warning Guadalcanal of impending air attacks—reporting 40 bombers and fighters on the 6th and a force of 36 Zeros the following day.

A chance also arose for getting the Catalina crew out of Bougainville, but the short time limit laid down by Station KEN prevented any hope of compliance. Briefly, a submarine had become available to attempt the rescue from Empress Augusta Bay. But, with only three days' notice, and the airmen at least a week away from the proposed evacuation spot, the chance had to be passed up for the time being.

A final effort to help us by propaganda means was made on the night I returned. Aircraft scattered more than 600 pounds of leaflets over the island. These notices warned the people of ultimate Japanese defeat, the folly of native sympathy toward the enemy, and the penalty of betraying Europeans. The leaflets were printed in simple Pidgin English and easily readable by the inhabitants. However, at this point, the propaganda raid was a bit too late. I think it would have been beneficial if done earlier. As regards my own little band of police, they derived their greatest incentive from radio talks broadcast in Pidgin English once a week via Port Moresby. Occasionally the speaker was a native well known to my men. We should have been doing more along these propaganda lines long ago.

On June 10, 1943, our situation in Bougainville was as follows. Dariai and Namatoa had been abandoned. The Catalina crew was escorted west, where a temporary camp was established at Sikoriapaia. Lieutenant Bedkober's detachment scouted the site looking for a location to evacuate the injured, and also for a suitable drop zone.

Sergeant McPhee (Station GIN) had moved to Kikiapaia, near Bedkober's unit, and seemed to be all right for the moment. Sub-Lieutenant Keenan (Station PLG) was safe and lying low behind Lumsis. Mason's party (Station NDT) was marking time in the vicinity of Empress Augusta Bay, pending reconnaissance to determine future plans. I stayed with Station BTU, and continued to operate the outpost forward of Aita. Sergeants Cohen, Broadfoot, and Radimey were quartered at the AIF base to my rear.

Rumors that the Japanese intended to penetrate the Aita area had been making the rounds for some time, so I gave no particular heed to the latest threat.

June 11 had been a pretty quiet day. The only visitor to our camp was the old chief of the village across from us on the other side of the Aita Valley. He had come to barter his produce for whatever we had to exchange. Our meager stock of trade items consisted of a twist of tobacco, some newsprint (coveted by the natives for smoke-paper [cigarette]), strips of cloth cut from parachutes, and salt. I remember that we paid him with newspaper and some fabric from the chutes. The chief headed homeward in the late afternoon. Although the village was only one air-mile from our base, the journey could not be made in less than four hours—a couple of hours to negotiate the steep descent to the Aita River, and the same length of time to climb up the other side.

At dusk we were warned that a strong Japanese force, accompanied by Numa Numa natives, was making its way inland along the banks of the Aita River. They had already passed the trail leading to our camp. Indications were that their objective might be the AIF base five miles farther upriver.

I was unable to warn the Army boys as my final scheduled transmission for the day had already been completed. Therefore I dispatched a couple of runners to try and get ahead of the enemy. I was not greatly concerned. I knew that Sergeant Cohen had the approaches to his position sufficiently covered to ensure adequate protection. Nor was I concerned about our own safety, for it seemed that the Japanese patrol had missed us. Nevertheless, in accordance with my usual policy, I ordered the teleradio dismantled and instructed the lads to hide the various components in the dense scrub surrounding the campsite.

We strengthened our guards and believed we had every possible access to our location secured. Constable Ena was in charge of the sentries posted farthest from the base. His men were positioned at the junction where the path coming up from the river joined the main track that skirted the crest of the valley and led to our camp.

Another sentry unit was set up about 50 yards down the main trail. Captain Robinson, Signalman Falls, and myself, along with a few police boys, prepared to take turns standing guard throughout the night. All hands were ready for any emergency at a moment's notice.

All was well at 9 P.M. when Signalman Falls went out to relieve Captain Robinson. Falls was standing guard with Sergeant Yauwika and my native servant, Womaru. Each man carried a couple of grenades and a .303 service rifle. A few yards in front of their position, the native boys placed a row of dry bamboo sticks, knee-high across the path. Anyone barging into them in the darkness would immediately alert the sentries.

Robinson had no sooner returned to camp when we were startled by a single rifle shot from the direction of Signalman Falls's post. A moment later, gunfire erupted on all sides. Robinson and I grabbed our weapons and dived for cover down the steep slope of the cliff. The next few minutes sounded like a battle royal being waged over our heads. The air was filled with the sounds of rifle volleys, exploding grenades, and the raking fire of machine guns.

From my position, only a few feet below the bluff, I watched the first rush of screaming Japanese and their native followers as they stampeded, like a herd of angry elephants, through the campsite. They fired their automatic weapons and tossed grenades indiscriminately. Our native boys had cleared out at the first shot—and Robinson and I were left alone.

The barrage of gunfire thrown up by the Japs indicated that they had attacked in force. They continued to rake the scrub with machine-gun bursts and grenades. But, fortunately, their attacks were not directed at our sector. However, that presented another potential problem. We imagined the possibility of another line of troops advancing in our direction. Fearing pursuit by native trackers, and the danger of our retreat being cut off at the river, we decided to try and sneak down the cliff and cross the Aita before dawn.

In the pitch blackness of night, we began the slow descent through the underbrush, making as little noise as possible and constantly on the alert.

We lay flat on the ground while slipping cautiously down the mountainside. I was unable to see Captain Robinson, but we kept in constant contact by touch. All around us, we could hear similar careful movements. I did not know until later that they were our own boys. After several minutes of working our way through the thick scrub, we found ourselves on what seemed to be the brink of a sheer precipice. Although we were still only a short distance from the camp, and mindful of our wide tracks through the underbrush, we had no alternative but to remain on the narrow ledge until dawn.

Meanwhile, above us, the Japs continued shooting into the bush. Every few minutes or so, their native followers would let out a yell as they discovered one of our caches. We put in a dark and dismal night listening to the enemy ransacking our base like a pack of mad wild dogs.

We were wise in having stopped when we did. Daybreak revealed that only a few inches separated us from a sharp drop of hundreds of feet. The horizontal ridge seemed to be never ending, but we had to risk going over the side. Crawling slowly and carefully over the ledge, we had moved about 50 feet down the cliff face when telltale pebbles began to tumble on us from above. Captain Robinson and I prepared to use our firearms. We had agreed never to be taken alive. Suddenly, I spotted one pair of brown legs after another cautiously feeling their way down the slope. Robinson decided that if his time was up, he was not going alone. He fired a rapid burst from his tommy gun. There was a scream, and another voice shouted out in Pidgin English, "Not to shoot—not to shoot!" The natives were a half-dozen of our own boys. Fortunately, the lad who was shot suffered only a flesh wound.

And so, the seemingly tragic turn of events developed into a favorable one for us. With our own natives as guides, we now stood a reasonable chance of escaping the enemy. But no time was to be lost in pushing on. The sound of shooting must have been audible at the camp. Continuing our descent, we soon reached a spot where it was impossible to go any farther. We were forced to remain where we were and hope for the best. The boys who found us reported that they had not seen or heard anything from the rest of our party since the enemy attack.

Throughout the day, while we sat huddled together on the rocky precipice, the pro-Japanese natives paraded along the top of the cliff—calling out the names of several of our lads, hoping they might reply and give our location away.

Late that evening, we climbed carefully back up to the top of the bluff, intent on moving farther along the crest of the mountain to hunt for an easier path down. Darkness foiled our search, however, and we hid in the bush until morning. At daylight, we broke through the thick undergrowth and skirted the mountain, finally reaching the Aita River by nightfall. Our party was now beginning to feel the pinch of two days without food. We had to reach a native garden as soon as possible. The common conception that a tropical jungle is glamorous and full of luscious fruits is as fallacious as it is popular.

We knew about the village that was up in the mountains across from our camp. Although Japs might still be in the vicinity, we had to take a chance on reaching the community gardens. Dawn the next day found us hacking our way through the brush and scaling the heights. When we arrived at the village, it was deserted. The inhabitants had fled at the first sound of gunfire. As we began to help ourselves to the garden vegetables, two of our missing police boys showed up—Sergeant Kanusi and Constable Iamulu. They had the same idea as we did, to confiscate some food. Sergeant Kanusi stated that, from his observation of footprints, he felt certain that Alan Falls and many of our natives had eluded the Japanese and escaped across the river. Their tracks headed in the direction of Aita.

We pulled up as many taro roots as we could carry and moved a safe distance from the village, then made camp and cooked our meal. I had never eaten taro before—even with all my years in the jungle. However, I now discovered that, baked in ashes, it was both flavorful and sustaining. It was a good thing I enjoyed the food, because taro roots were practically all we had to live on for six more long weeks.

The next morning, June 15, we learned that the Japanese had moved on to the west that previous afternoon. We decided to venture back to the campsite and see if the teleradio had survived the assault. The place had been burned to the ground. We lost everything, including supplies and personal gear. I located the batteries and power-charger to the wireless—they had been smashed to bits. However, the Japs had failed to find the transmitter, receiver, and speaker.

While searching the brush, we discovered the body of the old chief who had visited us on the day of the raid. When the enemy attacked, both Captain Robinson and myself believed that our lads had escaped before we did. However, one police boy stayed a few moments longer: Constable Iamulu, bent on greeting the person who betrayed us, and not caring who it might be, shot the first native he saw and then escaped in the brush.

Information later revealed that the chieftain was, in fact, responsible for the Japs learning our whereabouts. But the old man's actions were under duress rather than deliberate. The story, as I pieced it together, is that the chief, while crossing the river on the way back to his village, ran into several Numa Numa natives. The renegades were stragglers from the Japanese patrol. They apprehended the old man and took him to the commander of the enemy detachment. The chief was interrogated and probably threatened with death. The Japs wanted to know where he got the cloth and newspaper, both items now rare commodities on the island. In fear of his life, the chieftain pointed out our location and was forced to lead the enemy soldiers up the cliffs. Evidently, the old man also disclosed the position of Constable Ena's post, because the Japanese gave it a wide berth and emerged on the main trail close to our camp. The only thing that saved us was the secondary guard station. The Japs could very well have sneaked in without being noticed—and few, it any, of us would have survived.

We gathered up the unbroken components of the teleradio and headed for the Army base at Aita. I hoped to procure another engine, batteries, and fuel. I was also anxious to reassemble the rest of my routed party.

Okira [a servant] was the first person to greet us, and with ample food ready for everybody. He also had welcome news—Signalman Falls and other members of our group were safely hidden in the mountains nearby. Okira reported that, when the sounds of the raid echoed up the valley, he spirited the Chinese away to a secret hideout. He also stated that the Japs, after attacking the BTU station, hurried west without stopping at Aita. However, the AIF outfit dashed for the hills as soon as they heard the gunfire. Okira had not heard anything from them since.

The fact that the troops deserted their post did not really bother me. They probably expected to be next on the enemy's list. But I thought that the soldiers should have had enough time to put their house in order, so to speak, before abandoning the base. At the time of the assault on BTU, the Japs were at least two hours away from Aita. But the Army boys immediately fled into the jungle, leaving their equipment and stores behind. Captain Robinson and I fitted ourselves out with clothing, weapons, and gear. We found a power-charger in one of the AIF caches and retrieved a 12-volt battery from the wrecked Catalina.

On June 18, we joined Alan Falls and the rest of my party in the Aita mountains. However, I was still unable to get back on the air. I needed benzine to drive the charger but was hard-pressed to know where any was available.

Signalman Falls related his version of the attack on the wireless base. A few minutes after he had relieved Captain Robinson, someone was heard stumbling over the bamboo spikes. Thinking it might be one of our own lads returning along the trail, and unaware of the warning sticks, Sergeant Yauwika shouted a challenge. There was no reply. Falls, suspecting something was wrong, fired his rifle in the direction of the sound. Then all hell broke loose. A heavy barrage of enemy bullets cut wildly through the darkness. Falls and his boys stood their ground. They emptied their magazines and hurled grenades into the bush. Screams of pain indicated they had tossed a few strikes. However, the Japanese quickly brought a couple of light machine guns into action. Falls decided that this was a good time to get moving. He and his lads escaped down the mountainside to the river. They were joined by several others of our party, and the group headed for the Army base.

Native reports indicated that four enemy soldiers had been hit in the raid. Two dead bodies were dumped alongside the riverbank, while the wounded were carried back to Numa Numa on stretchers.

Jack Keenan showed up unexpectedly at our mountain hideout on June 19. He was accompanied by Corporals Little and McLeod. Their new campsite near Lumsis had been attacked on the 12th. They were forced to cache the teleradio to get out fast.

Keenan related his account of the incident:

We had just finished breakfast when machine-gun fire was heard some distance away. There were a number of aircraft about, and I thought, at first, that they were the ones doing the shooting. But suddenly we heard the rattle of more machine guns, followed by rifle shots. It was then I realized that the Japs were attacking our sentry post below the camp. Corporal Little immediately dashed to the base of the trail to give cover while we hid the wireless and other equipment.

About this time, a few of my scouts ran up from our lower camp. They informed me that a Japanese patrol, following the river, had sighted the outpost and opened fire. The shooting was getting closer, so McLeod and I took to the bush with only the supplies we could carry and headed west. At Aravia we linked up with Corporal Little and our police boys. They had escaped unharmed.

The next morning, we took the inland trail to Dariai, but found the camp burned and deserted. A party of natives, below the village, informed me that the Army lads had moved back to Aita, taking their stores and the Catalina crew with them. I was relieved to know the men were safe and decided to head after them.

The track between Dariai and Aita crosses a range about 2,000 feet high. The greater part of the path runs along razor-backed ridges. We were halfway up the northern slope when sounds were heard indicating that several people had left the trail in a hurry and dashed into the scrub ahead of us. My police boys knew they were natives and called to them. After a half hour, the lads came out of hiding and returned to the ledge. They were members of the BTU party and told me about the raid on Jack Read's post. I immediately decided to proceed over the ridge and up the Aita Valley to try and locate him.

When we reached the top of ridge near Aita, we discovered a dump of stores. We loaded up everything we could carry and continued down the mountain into the valley. Our forward scouts were reinforced and cautioned to be on the alert. After walking about 15 minutes, we came upon one of the BTU police boys who told me that Signalman Falls and a party of natives were hidden in the nearby bush. We were taken to the campsite and the following afternoon reached Jack Read's outpost.

My standing instructions to all coast watching stations were that if the enemy got too close, they should immediately withdraw to a place of complete safety and observe radio silence until the danger had passed.

I believe that Keenan was hampered in carrying out these orders—especially the part about moving to a safe location. On May 27, after the first Japanese attack on his base at Lumsis, he was left with a shortage of carriers. This was due to the natural inclination of the natives to panic at the sound of battle. Had he been able to travel several miles farther, he would have reached the mountainous headwaters of the Ramasan River. In all probability, the difficulty of access to that area would have deterred the enemy raid of June 12.

However, Keenan did have some good news. He had stashed a few quarts of benzine at Lumsis. I quickly sent two police boys to retrieve the fuel. This would be a very dangerous mission, but it was imperative that I get back on the air.

Because of the lack of communications, we were completely in the dark as to how the other coast watching bases were faring. I was also very much concerned about stores. The moon was reaching its zenith, and I wondered if Lieutenant Bedkober, at Sikoriapaia, had taken the initiative and arranged for a drop. I decided to send Keenan over there. Accompanied by Little and McLeod, he headed out from camp with instructions to reach the village as soon as possible and take charge of Station GIN. If Bedkober and his party were safe, Keenan was to contact Guadalcanal and coordinate a supply drop during the coming full moon.

Jack Keenan had no sooner departed than Sergeant V Day arrived with his detachment—and the tragic news concerning Bedkober's outpost. Sergeant Day reported his version of the disaster:

On June 1, 1943, Sergeant N. Martin, Pilot Officer Twist, and I left Aita with orders to locate a drop site near Sikoriapaia. After traveling all day, we made camp about halfway between the two villages. We contacted Lieutenant Bedkober on the portable radio and were instructed to remain where we were until additional help arrived.

On June 5, Sergeant Thompson and Corporal Wettenhall, of the Catalina crew, met us. We headed for Sikoriapaia to join Sergeant McPhee, who was operating Station GIN. However, upon arrival, we were notified that McPhee had moved his wireless outpost to Kikiapaia. We reached McPhee's location two days later, but found it unsuitable for a drop zone. I had learned that Japanese troops recently occupied Kunua. This bad news made any supply mission in the area too risky.

The following day, I decided to return to Sikoriapaia. Just as I was about to leave, Sergeants Collier and Martin and Airman Yates showed up. I assigned them to McPhee's post, and, taking Pilot Officer Twist and

Sapper Cassidy with me, hurried to meet Lieutenant Bedkober at Sikoriapaia.

The morning after we arrived, Bedkober and I traveled to a mission station near Kuraio, located south of the Kiviki River on the west coast. However, before reaching the mission we were informed by a native that the enemy was in force at Kuraio. It was too dangerous to go any farther, so we returned to the village.

On June 15, five airmen and seven soldiers were encamped at Sikoriapaia. Early the next day, while Lieutenant Bedkober remained with the injured airmen, I headed out to search the area for a safe drop site. Corporal Wettenhall and two soldiers accompanied me. We had only been gone about 45 minutes when we heard rifle and machine-gun fire coming from the direction of Sikoriapaia. Fearing the Japs had attacked the camp, we waited in the bush on the riverbank. After a couple of hours, a few of our police boys arrived and confirmed that a raid had been made on the base.

It would have been too hazardous to return to the village. The enemy was probably still in the vicinity. We moved cautiously east toward Aita. When we reached the Army camp, we were joined by Sergeants Radimey, Broadfoot, and Cohen. On the morning of the 19th, we met up with Sub-Lieutenant Keenan who was en route to Sikoriapaia. I told him about the attack on the outpost. Keenan then instructed us to proceed to Read's hideout, while he continued west to locate McPhee and somehow arrange for a supply drop.

Sergeant Day's party comprised ten men—somewhat of a problem for us to feed. There was nowhere in Bougainville that seemed particularly safe at the moment. The Japanese had struck our operation a savage blow from both east and west. I could do nothing at the present time but instruct Day to lead his group toward Dariai where food caches were known to exist. I told him to find a secure refuge in the area until he heard from me. Sergeant Day and his lads were also warned to attract as little attention as possible to themselves, as enemy patrols were reported to be in the Dariai-Aita vicinity.

A short time later, I learned from native scouts the story of what had actually happened at Sikoriapaia. At 10 A.M., on June 16, a strong force, believed to consist of 80 Japanese soldiers and 40 natives, stormed Lieutenant Bedkober's camp. This was probably the same patrol that attacked our BTU base and then continued westward. Stories of the raid are vague and lacking in detail. But, from information received, I compiled the following scenario: When the enemy charged the post, Flight Officer Dunn and Corporal Fenwick manned a Bren gun against the attackers, while Florance, Martin, Cassidy, Twist, and Yates fled into the bush. Local natives stated that Lieutenant Bedkober could also have escaped, but he preferred to stay with the injured airmen. In the firelight that ensued, Dunn was killed and Bedkober and Fenwick surrendered. Both men were carted off to the Kunua Plantation where they were placed aboard a schooner and taken to the Passage. It was later rumored that they had been moved to Inus. We never heard anything more about them after that.

Particulars concerning the fate of the five men who escaped are also sketchy. It is known that they made their way into the hills behind Numa Numa. But the lads had no food, only a few weapons, and some of them were barefooted. One account states that they were easily taken into custody by natives and handed over to the Japs. Another story contends they were captured by the enemy, then lined up and shot. However, the only definite information we have is that they fell into Japanese hands.

Our general opinion of Japanese procedure concerning prisoners of war in Bougainville was that, if you had the misfortune of being seized, your chances of survival were pretty slim.

On June 22, the boys I had sent to Keenan's camp returned with a few pints of benzine. It had been procured with great difficulty. The natives had to run the gauntlet of the Ramasan Valley, which was now being extensively combed by seven enemy patrols. By 7 P.M., BTU had built up enough capacity to break its prolonged silence and send a brief signal to Guadalcanal assuring headquarters of our safety. During the night, we worked hard on the engine, which was beginning to show signs of wear. The battery was also on its last legs. By morning, however, power had been increased enough to give us better transmission, and I was able to furnish Station KEN with more detailed particulars on our present status.

Messages received from Guadalcanal indicated that Sergeant McPhee, at Station GIN, had been maintaining irregular communications with KEN. McPhee later filled me in with additional information concerning his activities during the month:

About the first of June, I established my wireless base at Kikiapaia. Sergeants Collier and Thompson were with me. On the 15th, Lieutenant Bedkober visited our camp and asked me to move my station to his outpost the next day. On the morning of the 16th, we set out for Sikoriapaia. When we were within a few miles of the village, heavy firing was heard and burning huts were spotted. We sneaked in closer, for a better look, and sighted the Japanese force raiding the village. We immediately took refuge in the bush and remained hidden while enemy squads searched the area.

On the evening of June 17, I set up the teleradio and informed Guadalcanal of the attack on Sikoriapaia. KEN advised me that an evacuation was scheduled for sometime after June 22, and that there would be a supply drop of six parachutes on that night.

We spent the next four days in hiding and attempting to contact the other stations. During darkness, we gathered our equipment together and moved steadily toward the west coast. On the 22nd, we located a safe spot for the rescue and signaled KEN accordingly. The reply I received was very discouraging—the evacuation was placed on hold. My party was now in a desperate situation—we were out of food, and our wireless batteries were about gone. I urgently requested an emergency drop of a six-volt charger and provisions. My plan was to secure the drop and head back into the hills. I would then set up the wireless and send runners out to try and contact the other outposts. However, while waiting for the supply drop, my police boys met up with Sub-Lieutenant Keenan. He joined us and assumed command.

I could no longer ignore the unspoken thoughts that had literally imprinted themselves, like newspaper headlines, in my mind. After weighing the breakdown of our communication network, it was apparent that effective coast watching had, at long last, reached the end of its tether. We had enjoyed many good innings over a far longer period than anyone would have thought possible.

For more than a year, the self-opinionated Japanese soldier had allowed us to wage our kind of warfare against him—without any molestation other than mere threats to oust us from the island. We shall never know why he waited so long before cashing in on those threats. I can only attribute it to some lack of coordination in the Japanese hierarchy. However, the proof of our enemy's capabilities, once he started on the job, was now very much in evidence. The sons of Nippon had completely disorganized us, and they were not about to let up.

The aggressive assault by the Japanese against our positions was, of course, made easier by native alliance—the same methods we had used in our efforts to keep the loyalty of the village people. But more than 15 months of seemingly unhindered occupation by the enemy had swayed the Bougainville natives along their primitive cultural lines that "might is right."

The Japanese became increasingly preponderant, whereas we were but a mere handful. Rape, pillage, and murder were the blows that finally drove the wedge of conquest home. Practically the entire island was now pro-Japanese—and the morale of our own little band of natives was ebbing toward desertion.

On the grounds that we could be of no further use in Bougainville, and that any attempt to stay on would entail additional sacrifices to no useful purpose, I dispatched the following message to Guadalcanal on June 25:

> My duty is now to report that position of all here vitally serious. After 15 months occupation, almost whole island now pro-Japanese. Initial enemy patrols, plus hordes of pro-Japanese natives, have completely disorganized us. Position will not ease. Believe no hope to reorganize. Our intelligence value nil. In last fortnight, all parties have either been attacked or forced to quit. Reluctantly urge immediate evacuation.

Accompanying my request for a rescue operation, I also furnished particulars of our number—including the Chinese and my police boys who I could not leave behind. I suggested that a west coast rendezvous be selected.

Later that same afternoon, I was advised by Guadalcanal that Jack Keenan and his party had reached the west coast and he was in contact with KEN to arrange a stores drop. This supply mission would solve the food problem for Sergeant Day's personnel. They had not been faring too well as regards to provisions. Pro-Japanese natives had looted all the food caches in the Dariai area. Therefore, I instructed Day and his men to return west and link up with Keenan.

For several weeks, Captain Robinson and I had been entirely dependent on native foods. I sent Alan Falls, along with a group of police boys and carriers, to the drop zone. His orders were to await the shipment and then head back to our base with enough stores for everyone.

My wireless battery failed after my last signal to KEN, and we had very little benzine on hand. Boys who had been sent to Lumsis to obtain more fuel were held up by continued enemy activity in the Ramasan Valley. In any case, I dared not risk running the engine for fear its exhaust might attract the attention of the enemy. Japanese patrols were now making sweeps back and forth across the island. I do not believe that we were the object of these detachments, however. They were more in the nature of topographical survey parties. Their route usually followed either the top of the ranges or the river beds. This enemy activity went on for a couple of weeks, during which time the Japs also laid waste to every village and garden they came across. All we could do was wait and lie very low.

I did not get back on the air until July 13, when I was able to establish communications with both Guadalcanal and McPhee and learned what had occurred in the interim.

Sergeant Day crossed the island without mishap and joined up with Keenan on July 8. Day reported:

> I was advised that a supply drop was to be attempted that night. But also a party of Japanese were patrolling the beach a few miles away. We moved a short distance back into the bush and made camp. In the early morning hours of July 9, we heard the Catalina dropping the stores. By noon the next day, ten parachutes had been recovered, thus easing the food shortage considerably.

At this time, Sub-Lieutenant Keenan's group now comprised a total of 17 men, including Sergeant Thompson and Corporal Wettenhall from the crashed Catalina. Robinson and I were still hiding out in the Dariai vicinity. The seven Chinese were somewhere in the Aita mountains—only Okira knew their secret location. The police and the other natives I wanted to evacuate were distributed among the wireless parties.

I instructed Keenan to concentrate on trying to find information on the whereabouts of Paul Mason and his detachment. There had been no word from him for quite some time.

I entrusted two of my natives to find Okira and the Chinese men and bring them to Keenan's location. There were also a half-dozen married families and Bobby Pitt in hiding not too far from my base. I detailed other natives to escort these people across the mountains to the Kunua Plantation and to wait there pending further word from me.

Robinson and I proposed to break across country to the vicinity of Kunua and explore southward down the west coast for a suitable point of embarkation. Secrecy of movement was vital, and each party was to travel by different routes to minimize publicity.

On July 14, we were all en route westward as planned. The interior of Bougainville is as rugged and difficult as any I have ever encountered. We had to break bush and force our own trail over high mountain ranges—their precipitous peaks always shrouded in mists. While in the valleys, we hacked through almost impenetrable jungle growth. Our progress was much slower than we had anticipated. Food supplies ran out and we were unable to replenish—for that part of Bougainville is a no-man's land. Finally, on July 19, we cleared the mountain ranges and neared Kunua.

CHAPTER 12

The End of Attempts to Return to Southern Bougainville

MAY 1–JULY 19,1943

Paul Mason

On the first day of May 1943, Jack Read decided to send Lieutenant Keenan to supervise the Buka Passage area, and Lieutenant Stevenson and myself to southern Bougainville.

My instructions were to proceed to Dariai and collect a party of soldiers that had been assigned to us. From there we were to travel to Aita and pick up stores for the trip. I protested taking troops along on the journey, but Read insisted.

I have to speak critically of the eight soldiers who joined our expedition. They were too inexperienced and quite unsuited for the work required of them. It may be argued that I could have dispersed the Army lads in small patrol groups. However, conditions in the south were very much different than in Read's territory. If I had scattered the men, they would all have been lost.

It is difficult to lay down a specific set of instructions for coast watchers, because, in every locality, situations and natives differ. The new chum (or should I say chump) must learn, on his own, the pitfalls others have made and the experiences they have undergone.

When we reached Aita, there was some jealousy among the soldiers at the outpost, and at first they were reluctant to hand over the stores. In order to select a location for a supply drop during the next full moon, Stevenson and I went on ahead with the wireless equipment. Usaia Sotutu, ten police boys, and a half-caste, William McNicol, accompanied us. We left the troops at Aita. They were to remain there until I sent for them. Because it would have been impossible to travel secretly with such a large party—soldiers, police boys, and native carriers—I decided to strike across the island to Kuraio on the west coast and then continue south by canoe.

With the heavy equipment and provisions we carried, it was very difficult traversing the Emperor Mountains. After crossing the range at 5,000 feet, I attempted to contact Read as prearranged. However, I discovered that the teleradio vibrator had blown and the spare one was missing. After I had personally packed the wireless, the set had been interfered with by soldiers at Dariai. I sent a runner back to Sergeant McPhee at Aita requesting another vibrator. We then pushed on.

In the meantime, I directed Usaia to head for Kunua and collect several canoes. He met us at Kuraio, and we made our way by canoe down the west coast to Puruata. We traveled only at night, using sails to take advantage of the prevailing land breezes. During daylight hours, we hid the boats with brush and watched Japanese reconnaissance planes fly up and down the shoreline.

Upon landing at Puruata, I sent Usaia back to collect our party of soldiers. We learned that an enemy detachment had visited Puruata the day before we arrived and another patrol was due in about 24 hours. I noticed, inscribed on a wall at the deserted mission house, many Japanese-language characters, and also the words "Keep Out" in English. Underneath these words, Stevenson chalked his own message: "Like Hell."

From Puruata, we moved down the coast to Maravin. The Japs were reported to be three miles inland at Koari. We waited until they had cleared out and then moved in ourselves. We then traveled by canoe up the Reini River to a hill called Mom, which was surrounded by swamps. I decided to wait at this spot for the arrival of the vibrator and troops.

By this time, we had exhausted our eight-day supply of rations. The vibrator and soldiers were slow in coming. We had no means of communication, and, as the full moon began to wane, I realized that it was now too late for stores to be dropped by air.

All we needed was a vibrator, but the next day a native carrier showed up with a complete transmitter from Lieutenant Bedkober. Read was never informed about the broken equipment, nor did he know for some time that Bedkober had actually sent the Numa Numa transmitter to me.

The eight soldiers arrived about the same time. They had walked down the western shore while the rest of our supplies followed them at night by canoe. These guys had been having a great time as they leisurely meandered along the coast. Under the sharp eyes of Japanese pilots, these raw troops had been joyriding in native canoes, tossing hand grenades in the water to catch fish, and shooting their rifles for sport.

They were the same men who, before we left Aita, Stevenson had lined up and instructed on how to behave in this primitive environment:

> Remember, the natives look to the white man for leadership. Always maintain the white man's reputation for fairness and justice. If you give the natives your word, keep it, but do not become too familiar with the people. Do not waste your ammunition and hand grenades or fire rifles for fun. Keep out of sight from enemy aircraft and do not hang around Kuraio.

Every one of these orders was disobeyed.

Besides a sapper, a private, and three careless signalmen, the Army lads included three sergeants—one in charge of the detachment, one in charge of supplies, and one who thought he should be in charge of everything.

I had emphatically instructed the signal boys to keep their portable radios dry at all costs, attesting to the fact that these units might save their lives in the bush. However, only one of the soldiers, Signalman G. Kotz, showed any interest in the equipment. His was the only unit that reached Mom in working order. The dry batteries of the other sets were sodden wet and useless.

Although the troops had set out with a month's supply of rations, they plodded into camp without any food after traveling for only ten days. Lieutenant Bedkober had selected these men, reported to be his best soldiers. Two of them, a chronic complainer and a fellow with only one eye, had been on the island a month. The others were recent arrivals from the last submarine trip.

Stevenson and I gave the "country club" gang a good dressing down and put them on short rations for a while—but we never trusted the Army bunch out of our sight again. To give these lads their just due, however, they were later to stand up well under fire, as long as Stevenson and I were in sight, but there was not one leader among them. They remained a perpetual worry to me, especially after Lieutenant Stevenson's death.

A lot of time had already been wasted, and it was imperative to find a permanent location for the wireless. Therefore, I stayed at Mom with four soldiers, a few police boys, and William McNicol. Stevenson, Usaia Sotutu, and the rest of our party scouted the countryside.

The Japanese had been showing a great deal of interest in the coastal belt of Empress Augusta Bay. The region was flat with numerous waterways. But large sandbars, at the mouth of the rivers, prevented the passage of enemy barges. Our outpost at Mom seemed relatively safe, and I was able to view the coastline from Puruata to Mutapina Point.

We had a couple of scares while waiting for Lieutenant Stevenson to return. Rumors stated that a Japanese force was preparing to investigate the Mom vicinity. I decided to move to a nearby hill to watch for enemy patrols and ambush them if necessary. We waited in the bush for most of the day. Finally, just before dusk, a party of nine Nips was sighted reconnoiter-ing the area. However, there was only one rifle amongst them. As a matter of course, and in order not to disclose our presence, I let the group move on undisturbed. I suspect that the Japs, knowing we were not an offensive threat, deliberately sent out lightly armed parties for scouting and observation purposes.

For the past month, we had been living on food from native gardens. This vegetable diet was supplemented by fish and an occasional wild pig. I also managed to condense salt from seawater. William McNicol did most of the foraging. We received one supply drop during the period, but the Catalina released his parachutes from an altitude of 2,000 feet instead of the usual 500. Two chutes were recovered. The others drifted into the jungle and were never found.

George Stevenson showed up around the middle of June, but I was surprised to see that he was alone. He had located a wireless base above Iru, about 25 miles to the southeast. George had discovered that his soldiers were too much of a hindrance and dropped them off at Reira. Usaia Sotutu was directed to look after the Army boys. Stevenson placed Constable Buia in charge of the natives and left them at the teleradio site. He then traveled by himself to Mom.

On June 17, Lieutenant Stevenson and I set out for Iru with my detachment, the wireless equipment, and our supplies. We traveled ten miles inland along a river. The journey upstream was more arduous than expected. We were forced to spend two nights in swamp country where mosquitoes made sleep impossible. The next evening we beached the canoes and moved inland from the marshes. I decided to leave Stevenson and my four soldiers to guard the supplies while I headed with the teleradio and a few police boys to Reira. I was able to obtain additional carriers on the trail and sent them back to Stevenson's camp to haul the stores.

I arrived at Reira on June 21 and was greeted by Usaia and the other Army lads. Lieutenant Stevenson and the supplies showed up late in the afternoon. The following day, in a heavy rainstorm, I set out with half our force toward Iru. That evening, friendly natives reported that the Japs had summoned all the village chiefs and prominent people of the area to Japanese headquarters at Mosigetta. They were assembled to witness the execution of several native carriers who had helped us.

On the 23rd, I pushed on to Dubonemi and camped above the village. Stevenson arrived later in the day. George related that his party had come across a few unarmed enemy scouts, but he was able to prevent his soldiers and carriers from panicking. That evening, one of the natives who had been stationed at Iru, met us with news that the Japs had raided the campsite and taken Buia prisoner. They also seized our gear and packs.

Because of the executions at Mosigetta, the Navarissi villagers turned against us, and it became necessary to find a safe defensive location. We immediately headed to Ossiangi and waited for a supply drop. All the chutes, but only one dump, were recovered. Surrounding our party with scouts, we moved up into the central Crown Prince Range. I posted strong guard units at each halt. On the 24th, we received word that our previous night's campsite had been raided and stores we had cached were found by the enemy.

We proceeded higher and more deeply into the mountains and established a temporary base along a ridge that could be easily defended. There was no point in heading to Iru. I planned to cross the watershed and move down to the upper reaches of the Luluai Valley. By now it was impossible to recruit native carriers. We had to rely on our own boys who could only haul half the remaining stores at a time.

My party had become too large and unwieldy. I decided to split the group into two units. I instructed Stevenson to remain on the ridge with Sergeant Furner, Signalmen E. Rust and A. Eastlake, Usaia Sotutu, and my best police boys. I continued along the trail with Sergeant Thorpe, Signalman Kotz, Private H. Woods, William McNicol, and enough natives to carry the wireless. When I located a safe location, I planned to send the carriers back to Stevenson. He would then bring his men and our supplies to the camp.

Climbing to 6,000 feet, I led my party across the range. After locating a good site southwest of Moru, I sent the carriers back for Stevenson. The next morning, a cook-boy rushed into our camp with news that Japs had attacked Stevenson's location and that George had been shot. The cook-boy took off as soon as the firing began.

The following is what apparently occurred: The ridge upon which Stevenson and his men were situated was joined to the mountain by a sheer wall of rock. A steep cliff protected one flank of the ledge, while paths snaked up the other side of the bluff. The first trail was the one by which we had arrived at the site, and the second was the path I had taken to cross the main range. However, there was also a third track that I discovered when we reached the ridge. This path led down to a hiding place where local natives kept their women in time of danger.

The three trails accessed the ledge through dense thickets of bamboo. During the time that I was with Lieutenant Stevenson, guards were posted at each track, and the paths were blocked with dry bamboo sticks.

On the morning of June 27, Stevenson and his men went down the first trail to wash in the nearest stream and then returned and had lunch. While they were taking an after-lunch nap, a shot range out: the Japs were on the ridge. An enemy patrol had sneaked up the third path, which was left unguarded during daylight hours.

Stevenson had been resting in an open shelter made of banana leaves and located near the track used by the approaching Japanese. He spotted the Nips, but before he could reach for his Austin gun, he was shot through the heart. A native who was with him tried to grab the weapon, but George had fallen on top of it. Meanwhile, Usaia's rifle jammed. He also attempted to get the Austin gun, but was unable to move Stevenson's body.

Although our lads were taken by complete surprise, they managed to regroup and open fire on the enemy. What actually happened next is unclear, except the fact that five Japs were killed. Leaving everything behind but their rifles, the soldiers and police boys escaped over the second path and joined me near Moru.

While fleeing the enemy, they came across a native who had been propagandizing the local people and had helped the Japanese locate Stevenson's camp. The traitor begged for his life, saying that Buia had only been imprisoned, and that the five Japs killed on the ridge were enough people for one day. My lads thought not—and executed him on the spot.

On June 28, I sent two police boys back to the ridge to bury Stevenson and reconnoiter the area. They found the body, stripped of clothing, some distance down the cliff. The natives had no tools to dig a grave, but they laid out the corpse and covered it with a shroud of banana leaves. The police noticed that the bodies of the dead Japanese and the traitor had been taken away.

My party was now in serious trouble. We had no benzine to charge the radio batteries and very little food. Our circumstances were such that we were forced to keep moving to locate native gardens and elude the Japs at the same time. But, our heavy wireless equipment impeded our progress in any direction.

However, I still had enough battery power to last a short time. I contacted Guadalcanal and advised them of my plight. I received an immediate signal back stating that, within a few day's time, we would receive a supply drop at Kereaka.

I was stunned. Kereaka was on the west coast—a good three weeks forced march from Moru. I immediately telegraphed an urgent message back that it was impossible for us to reach the site in time for the proposed drop and that I wanted to continue my mission and set up a coast watching outpost in southern Bougainville. I knew the area like the back of my hand.

My pleading went for naught. I was ordered to proceed immediately with the teleradio to Kereaka. Sergeant McPhee was in the area and had been advised of our trouble. I was reluctant to abandon the attempt to reach Buin, but realized that, without my help and direction, the soldiers would never live to join McPhee.

On June 29, we set out for the far west. I was unable to contact local natives to ascertain the whereabouts of enemy patrols. Whenever we stopped at a village garden to collect food, not one person approached us. I suspected that every native was now watching our movements on behalf of the Japanese. I really wanted to cache the radio. Carrying it with us endangered our chances of survival. But I toted it along in accordance with instructions.

We advanced in column, heading cautiously westward toward Meridau. I split my party into three units. Two scouts moved out ahead of the first group, which comprised four soldiers, William McNicol, and myself. The carriers and police boys followed with the teleradio. Sergeant Hatherly, three other soldiers, and Usaia Sotutu brought up the rear. I did not expect an attack from this quarter, but I instructed Hatherly that, if one did occur, he was to hold off the enemy until I moved the wireless to a safe spot. If the assault came from the front, I would protect the column while the rear guard hid the radio equipment. I impressed on the soldiers the necessity of avoiding panic at any cost.

While we were crossing the gorge at Meridau, our scouts disturbed a group of Japanese in the village above us. The Nips quickly opened fire with rifles, grenades, and a machine gun. I hustled my party off the trail and into the bush. We immediately began shooting up at the enemy. A soldier near me did not have a weapon. I gave him my revolver. The machine gun raked our position from a small hut and had us pinned down for several minutes. I directed my police to concentrate their fire on the hut and the gun was soon silenced. But there was no time to relax. Suddenly four Japs charged down the slope. Before they came within range of my tommy gun, a police boy dropped one of them. Without waiting to pick up the body, the others fled into the village.

Believing that Hatherly had hidden the wireless set, I gave the order to fall back. A couple of police covered our retreat. As we withdrew, I spotted the battery charger lying alongside the path. Private Woods and I, although carrying full packs ourselves, managed to lug it downhill. But, that was not my only surprise. When we reached the bottom of the gorge, I discovered the food box. It had also been abandoned—even though it contained our only rations, which had to last us for the next three weeks, plus tobacco we had saved for bartering purposes.

I collapsed with rage and exhaustion. Leaving the charger and food box, I went to search for the fugitive members of our party. I found them an hour later, huddled like a bunch of frightened sheep along a path in the gorge. When the shooting started, the carriers dumped the teleradio and stores. The panic-stricken natives told Sergeant Hatherly that I had fled downstream and then they took off up the gorge. The battery, transmitter, and receiver to the wireless were never found.

Sergeant Thorpe, the one-eyed soldier with a skull and crossbones tattooed on his chest, dropped his pack and bolted. The pack carried by this so-called commando contained several bloodthirsty props, including a knuckle-duster and a knife.

I gathered my party together as fast as possible and headed rapidly down the gorge. At nightfall, while I was leading the group up the rocks, hunting for a flat place to make camp, a shot rang out. Thinking the Japs had caught up with us, we hit the dirt, only to discover that a round had been fired from Signalman Kotz's rifle. He had been carrying the weapon with a cartridge in the breech. The safety catch had worked loose and the trigger was shocked.

It is always dangerous to carry a rifle in this manner—especially in the jungle. I had warned the troops repeatedly to carry their guns at half cock if they wanted a round in the breech. But now it was too late, a nearby village had definitely been alerted.

Hatherly, Woods, and I were now the only men with packs. The others had either lost theirs or tossed them away. Of such stuff were these soldiers made.

Without food or cover, the party slept in the open under pelting rain. I distributed my own blankets, and such stores as I could spare, to the unfortunate lads who were without (two days later these blankets were lost). For breakfast, we had very little indeed.

Throughout the next day, we continued moving down the gorge, climbing up cliffs, over huge boulders, and gradually wearing ourselves out. We made camp at dusk, and I sent my police boys out to forage for food. They did not return until morning, but then we had a feast—taro, yams, and green bananas.

During the night, while the boys were busy plundering the garden of a native village, the inhabitants were locked in a violent argument—trying to decide whether or not they should assist the Japs in our pursuit.

We were still proceeding down the gorge on the morning of July 2. The going was extremely rough, but toward midday the terrain widened out into a narrow valley. We were probably not far from Lamparan. We had not gone far when my scouts returned with news that three natives were up ahead and on the lookout for us. I had my party fan out. Creeping forward, unobserved, we managed to grab two of the natives, but the third escaped. The captured pair were brothers. The older boy, who could speak Pidgin English, at one time had worked for Fred Archer. The younger lad, not more than a child, was obviously very frightened. They denied that they had been looking for us on behalf of the Japanese. I asked them why native drums had been beating all morning. The older lad replied that their chief was summoning carriers for a Jap patrol that was traveling to Kieta. I instructed the younger boy to return to his village and tell the people that his brother was being held as a hostage. Then I told the other lad that unless he agreed to lead us out of Negavisi territory, we would treat him as a Japanese spy.

Our hostage wanted to take us to his village, but, fearing a trap, I declined. He then led us through the bush and skirted the settlement. In the meantime, his younger brother must have reached home. In the distance we could hear the howling and wailing of women, and the beating of drums intensified. After traveling for a while in what seemed to be circles, the

hostage said that we were approaching a main trail. I informed
the lad that this path was too dangerous and indicated the way
we desired to head. However, the boy reported that it was
blocked by an impassible ridge. We returned to the river valley.
The hostage agreed to guide us to a track leading out of the
gorge and in the direction we wanted to go. My party now consisted of eight soldiers, Usaia Sotutu, William McNicol, six
police boys, and a dozen native carriers.

Reentering the narrow valley, the soldiers and I kept close
to the cliff edge, protected by large rocks and brush. The
natives preferred the easier going of the riverbed. We had not
walked very far when enemy fire erupted. The carriers dashed
across the stream to safety, while we hit the deck. As soon as the
shooting started, our hostage made a break for home. The
police boy, who had been guarding him, fired two rounds after
the fleeing lad, but he escaped. I instructed my men to hold
their fire until they could see the enemy. However, the Japs
never appeared.

After the shooting ceased, we remained undercover for
some time. When I finally reassembled my party, William McNicol, Constable Kiabai, and ten carriers were missing. We continued carefully down the valley and soon came upon a
recently cleared trail. I ordered my group to hide in the brush
and stay quiet.

A few minutes later, three Japanese scouts, possibly decoys,
were sighted sneaking down a nearby hill and moving toward
our position. They passed close to us and then headed up the
path. The Japs returned about dusk, swaggering along the trail
and shooting off their rifles indiscriminately. I believe they
were trying to draw our fire, or else drive us into a pocket
where we could be surrounded.

It began to rain about dusk. I decided to stay put until
dark. Just before nightfall, we sighted 16 enemy soldiers heading up the path in the direction of the hill. About 7 PM., using
a luminous compass, I led my party silently across the trail.
Each man had been instructed to attach a piece of phospho-

rescent fungus to his body in order to enable those behind to keep contact in the dark.

We plodded along for an hour or so, stumbling and falling in the pouring rain. After finally reaching a stream, I found a level spot in the brush along the bank and decided to call a halt to our march. Everyone was exhausted. For the rest of the long night, we lay side by side and back to back, huddled together for warmth.

The following morning, July 3, having had no food for 24 hours, we once again continued our journey across country. I set a compass course for the ridge above Reira. I intended to cross the ridge at a point north of Koro, the principal track between the east and west coast. We kept a careful lookout for Japs. All packs, except my own, were now lost. The only food I carried, an Australian emergency ration, I divided between the men.

While we were pushing our way west, several of the natives we lost in the valley ambush showed up. They had tracked our footprints through the bush. They reported no news of either William McNicol or Kiabai.

During the afternoon, we found a village garden and stocked up on vegetables. We located a safe place to make a fire and had our first meal in 36 hours. After filling up on baked taro, we resumed the trek to Reira. For a day and a half, we had tramped through the jungle barefooted. However, after robbing the garden, I knew we could not conceal our tracks from the native villagers, so we put our boots back on.

Late in the afternoon, we stopped in the bush to rest while waiting for scouts to signal an all clear. Suddenly a Japanese soldier was spotted pedaling his bicycle about 30 yards ahead. Until that moment, I had not realized how near we were to the main trail. Some of the troops foolishly ducked, but I remained immobile until the Jap passed.

A short time later, our scouts signaled us to cross the road. We soon reached a high bluff to our front. I decided to wait until nightfall before attempting to climb the cliff. At dark we began to scale the steep slope. Our bodies were soon scratched and torn by lawyer vine. As I crawled upwards, the grade became more vertical and the undergrowth much thicker. We reached a narrow ledge near the summit and elected to spend the night on the cliff. To keep from rolling downhill, each man scooped out a step in the side of the slope. Far below, I could see the bright fires of a Japanese camp. Rain started to fall. The cold became intense, and few of us slept.

At daybreak, July 4, I discovered that we were dug in on a peak rising from the Reira Ridge, but still a good distance from Reira itself. It was impossible to continue the climb, so we made our way along the ledge until I found a path leading over the range. When we reached Reira, the village was deserted, and we helped ourselves to the gardens. The Japanese were just over the ridge at Moro, so we moved down to the Jaba River where we cooked the food and made camp for the night. Sentries were posted and we all managed to get a good sleep.

The next day, we passed through Tobruata. The local natives were sullen and close-mouthed, but I felt fairly safe. We were unable to obtain any food at the village and left hoping to find gardens farther along the route.

I seemed to tire faster than the younger members of the party. But we were all weak to some extent from lack of proper food and overexertion. We averaged two meals of native vegetables each day—but without salt. Toward evening, we reached a deserted village on the Tekassi River and collected food from the gardens. The next day, I shot a one-eyed pig and trapped another one alive. That night, we had our first meat in a week. While we were enjoying the feast of roast pig, one of our missing carriers arrived. He brought Wood's haversack with him and was quite proud of his achievement. The native also carried a note for me, purported to have been signed by the commander of the Japanese Army. The message [written in imperfect English] was undated and written on a sheet of paper that had been removed from one of the lost packs. It read:

MY DEAR ANSACS

WE JAPANESE TROOPS ADMIRE FOR YOUR BRAVE ACTS. YOU HAVE ALL DONE YOUR BEST FOR THE GLORY OF GREAT BRITON.

BUT NOW YOU ARE SURROUNDED BY OUR ARMY TROOPS. ANYWHERE YOU GO, YOU WILL SEE THE EYE OF WATCHING. YOU HAVE DROPPED IN TRAPS LAID BY US. ALL THE SMALL ROAD AND JUNGLE ARE NOW WATCHING BY OUR SOLDIERS AND THE MORE SHARPER EYE OF THE NATIVES. ALL YOUR ATTEMPTS TO RUN AWAY OR TO GO IN TOGETHER WITH OTHER YOUR TROOPS IN BUKA ARE IN VAIN.

NOW YOU CAN ONLY WAITING DEATH OF HUNERY [hunger] IN THE JUNGLE. NOW SOME OF YOUR CAMERADS HAS BEEN SACRIFICED AND CAUGHT BY US. YOU MAY FEAR FOR CRUELLY OF JAPANESE TROOPS BUT WE ARE NOT CRUEL. THIS IS PROVAGANDA OF U.S.A. OFTEN SPEAK ILL OF US. WE DARE ADVICE TO YOU—SURRENDER TO US!! COME TO US AND YOUR ALIVES SHALL BE KEPT ALIVE ASSUREDLY

CAPTAIN ITO

JAPANESE TROOPS

The fellow who delivered this note to me stated that he received it from another native, who told him that the Japs had captured Usaia Sotutu. However, as Usaia was still with my party, I concluded that the enemy had captured, and probably killed, William McNicol, mistaking him for Usaia.

I took little notice of the rigmarole nonsense calling upon us to surrender. However, the message confirmed my belief that our "friends in Buka" were still free, which helped our morale considerably.

On July 7, we headed down into the swamp country behind Mom and Koari, where we met a group of friendly natives.

They complained to me that the Japanese had destroyed their gardens and also warned us that the enemy was encamped at Mom. That night, they led us through the dark swamplands to a village near Maravin. These natives were lifesavers. We were able to eat and sleep in peace for a change.

I had been feeling very weak, but after a day's rest my strength began to improve. However, the tense strain of the journey was taking its toll on the Army lads. The health of the soldiers deteriorated, and their nerves were beginning to fray. But this was no time for petty grievances. I assembled my party, gave them a lecture, and pushed on. We crossed the flat land behind Puruata and, on the night of the 10th, camped on the bank of the Laruma River. We were not far from the principal track crossing the island from Puruata to Numa Numa. I expected this path to be heavily patrolled and, sure enough, we received word that the Japanese had been along the road that afternoon.

The next morning, we followed a trail along the river that wound around Kuvi Mountain. I learned the Japs had passed that way the day before. About dusk, we came upon deserted gardens in a village near the river. We cooked our dinner and camped for the night.

The track we had taken zigzagged toward the west coast and through the rugged limestone mountains of the Emperor Range. The journey was difficult, dangerous, and monotonous. Despite increasing fatigue, we were forced to climb again and again to heights of 5,000 feet—then plunge downward to the dry river courses between the peaks. Hiking through continual tropic rainstorms and having no blankets for the cold, we slept at night alongside our fires, letting the smoke dry out our clothes.

The scattered villages in this high country had heard about the war and Japanese atrocities, but the people had never seen a Jap—and, most of them had not even seen a white man. I was asked at one village whether we were Japanese or English. I replied "English," and we were invited to help ourselves to the gardens.

I appeared very thin at this time. But, apart from festering cuts and scratches, I was in good shape. On the other hand, several of the soldiers were in poor condition. Woods had a high fever. Furrier suffered with an ugly abscess on his thigh. Rust was troubled with an ulcerated leg, and Eastlake was becoming weaker by the day. Sergeant Thorpe, who had always been a bother to us on the march, was as fit, if not fitter, than I—a fact I attribute to his scrounging food from Usaia and the police boys. Thorpe had more to eat than any of us.

On July 16, I gave the party a rest from their daily climbing. We learned from native sources that unidentified soldiers were a day's march away. I sent two police boys ahead to investigate. I gave them only a verbal message to relay and no written note.

Two days later, a couple of natives showed up carrying tea, meat, and a message from Lieutenant Keenan. He had kept my two exhausted police boys with him. I decided to push on alone and meet Keenan. I reached his camp at Kereaka that night. Already assembled at the site were McPhee, the rest of the Army detachment, and the survivors of the Catalina crash. The next day, July 19, my group was guided to Keenan's location.

I was informed that a submarine would arrive in about five days and evacuate us. Jack Read, however, was still several days from the west coast and planned to leave the island on a second trip. I sent Usaia and my best police boys to assist Read in his journey to the evacuation site.

A COMMENT BY KEN THORPE

Sergeant Ken Thrope, who still has the original letter to Paul Mason, recalls its arrival:

My personal carrier arrived at camp with my pack [Mason wrote that the pack belonged to Private Woods] and handed me a letter written by the Japanese Commander. I was so affected after receiving a note on my own paper that I jumped up—waved my tommy gun in the air, and shouted, "Come and get us!"

CHAPTER 13

The Death of Admiral Yamamoto and the Ambush of Mason's Party

MARCH 29–JUNE 26, 1943

Ken H. Thorpe and Walter Radimey

Ken Thorpe was part of an Army detachment headed by Lieutenant D. Bedkober that landed on Bougainville on March 29, 1943. During the first week of April, Thorpe and a few other members of the detachment left Namatoa and headed south on a scouting mission with Usaia Sotutu as their guide. Ken Thorpe, at 70 years of age, still vividly remembers his canoe trip down the coast of Empress Augusta Bay:

After reaching Namatoa, our detachment was split into three parties, each consisting of eight soldiers and a number of trusted natives. I also met Usaia Sotutu—a fine stamp of a man, six feet tall or over, whose wife Margaret and young children passed me as our boat, from the U.S.S. *Gato*, headed for the beach. Mrs. Sotutu, and her children, were on their way to safety aboard the submarine. I was among the first 12 Army personnel that arrived on this trip [March 29, 1943]. The *Gato* returned to Brisbane and came back a month later with the other 12 members of our unit. We had all trained together in Australia.

The group to which I was attached was under the command of Paul Mason. We traveled toward the west coast of Bougainville, intending to proceed south in hopes of establishing an observation post as close as possible to the Kahili airfield—and also overlooking Kieta and Numa Numa.

With the exception of myself, the other soldiers journeyed by land, following the coastline of Empress Augusta Bay. I went by sea on a large war canoe, packed with stores and ammunition. We sailed about 40 miles and, during this period, eight Japanese planes flew over us at various times. Each aircraft dived on the canoe at masthead height to inspect our craft. The natives covered me with a platform, and Usaia Sotutu stood on top. The natives shipped their paddles and pretended to be fishing. They madly waved friendly greetings at the scrutinizing planes. I felt that I was the luckiest man in the world. I thought for sure that the enemy would fire on us just for sport. On our way down the coast we caught a 23-pound kingfish.

We reached the Puruata Mission before the boys that were taking the land route arrived. The stove in the two-story mission building was still hot from a Jap patrol that had used it earlier in the day. I stoked the smoldering fire and prepared to cook the fish. A short time later, the rest of our detachment showed up—their feet cut to pieces by the sharp volcanic sand that had worked its way into their boots. A dozen days on the submarine with no exercise, coupled with soft food (hotcakes, syrup, sweet corn, spam, and all the other wonderful food on the *Gato*), had made us unaccustomed to the rations we trained on. None of the lads were fit to travel any farther, so we posted sentries and rested for 24 hours.

The following day, I proceeded with the Army boys south along the beach of Empress Augusta Bay. There was a heavy surf running. Suddenly, two Zeros were spotted. They traced the coastline at palm tree height and we made a wild dash for cover. Minutes later, an American Avenger or Wildcat rounded Puruata Point, turned right, accelerated, and scurried off in the direction of Rabaul. If this plane had been a Jap, we would not have had time to hide. The thick jungle growth absorbs the sound of motors to such a degree that an aircraft is upon you before it can be heard.

The rest of our trip down the coast was without incident. Eventually we made our way inland along a riverbank. Using canoes, we crossed to the other side and followed a track to a native village. We waited there for Paul Mason. We were now entering hostile territory and many Japanese patrols had been reported in the vicinity.

While waiting at the village, three of us walked back to the coast. We spent the day boiling seawater to condense salt, which we would need in order to continue our journey. We were returning to the village and had just reached a bend in the river when machine-gun fire opened up. We dove for the bush and hit the ground. I quickly realized that all the shooting was coming from an aerial dogfight taking place over our heads. I noticed an American P-38 and a Japanese "Betty" bomber weaving in and out of the low cloud cover. Machine-gun bullets and cannon shells (from the P-38) began splattering the brush on all sides of us. We decided it was time to get out of the area before we got killed, and we were lucky to make it back to camp alive. I later learned that this air battle was the one in which Admiral Yamamoto was shot down.

When we landed on the island to relieve Lieutenant Mackie's section, the handwriting was on the wall. The Japs were becoming bolder and were able to find natives who would lead them into the mountains. We also had dogs to contend with, which made our work that much harder. [Jack Read claimed that he was never chased by dogs.]

Before one of the Catalina drops, I asked Paul to order a case of red pepper. I would sprinkle it around whenever we left a village or campsite. It sure confused the dogs and set the enemy back a bit.

Walter "Lucky" Radimey, who also was a member of Lieutenant Bed-kober's detachment, remembers the Catalina crash:

On or about the 28th of April 1943, one of two Catalinas attempting to drop us supplies of food and ammunition crashed. We searched all night, and the plane was found just after dawn. We rescued six out of the crew of nine. The pilot, copilot, and drop-master were killed in the accident.

We were unable to release the bodies of the pilot and copilot, as the plane was upside down and the men were pinned in the cockpit. The forward part of the aircraft and its two motors were pushed back. The body of the drop-master was jammed underneath the Catalina. Fuel had spilled all over the crash site.

The six survivors were all injured—four seriously. I had my hands full taking care of them. The Japanese located the PBY [Catalina] some time after the crash. And, whenever enemy troops were in the area, they would use the wrecked plane for target practice. From time to time, the Japs would "stake out" the crash site for some unknown reason.

This background is relevant for a number of reasons. The location of the Catalina crash was in the same general vicinity of where Admiral Yamamoto was shot down. One of our parties, on the southern part of the island [see Sergeant Thorpe's report], saw and heard the air battle and was subjected to strafing. Some of us, in central Bougainville, also witnessed the dogfight, but we did not know what it was all about.

Shortly after the aerial engagement, we received a signal asking us to search for an American fighter pilot who was also shot down in the same area. A number of parties were sent out on "search and find" missions. However, the search had to be abandoned since there were too many Jap patrols in the vicinity. They were probably hunting for either Yamamoto or the American aviator.

We were later informed (although I cannot verify the story) that when Yamamoto was eventually found, his body was in a reasonable state of preservation. A bullet hole was in the back of his head, supposedly fired by his adjutant or aide.

Several years ago, I accidentally came across an article that was titled "Waiting for Help That Never Came." The gist of the story was that a bush-walking party on Bougainville found a skeleton in a sitting position leaning against a tree (somewhere in the general area of the Catalina crash). Both legs were broken, but the skeleton still had side arms strapped on and dog tags were attached to the body. The remains were identified as those of the American pilot who was shot down in the Yamamoto incident.

Following is Ken Thorpe's version of the events leading up to Lieutenant Stevenson's death and of the Japanese ambush of Mason's party while attempting to cross the gorge at Meridau:

The native carriers we hired to haul our gear up the mountains came from a village we passed through on the afternoon of June 25. Although they seemed a bit suspicious, we desperately needed carriers and paid them extra-well—a twist of tobacco and a pipe for each man.

That night, we all took our turn at guard. The mountain air was very cold. Usaia and I built a platform of green bamboo, about two feet above the ground, and lit a smoke fire underneath. The next morning, Sergeant A. Hatherly and myself, along with Constable Kiabi, scouted down the other side of the mountain toward the Luluai River. We carried some food and gear with us. After traveling a few hours over very rough terrain, we came across a deserted village on the edge of a sheer cliff. The compound comprised six or seven huts, two of them built on high piles. A palisade of closely grown bamboo surrounded the village, and the only entrance was a small eye-of-the-needle gate. The area in front of the barricade was open ground, with the exception of many small bushes. The cliff, to the rear of the village, dropped off into a very steep gorge. When Paul Mason arrived with the rest of our party later that day, we made camp for the night.

Unfortunately, the overpaid carriers decided to return to their village and were intercepted by the Japanese, who noticed the pipes and tobacco. Probably under threat of death, they led a Nip patrol to where we had left Lieutenant Stevenson and his men. George was killed, and the enemy destroyed the camp-site—shooting holes in our cooking utensils and cans of bully beef.

The members of Stevenson's party who fled the surprise attack met us at the village. They were dog-tired and carried only their weapons. After a meal of Army rations and a bit of taro, the exhausted men bedded down for the night.

I took my turn as sentry that evening, just outside the narrow gate of the compound. It was very dark and I could hear the mournful wailing of Japanese tracking dogs tied up across the river. The lonely vigil of guard duty plays tricks with the imagination. I was positive that the small bushes to my front were moving ever so slowly toward me. I automatically put one hand over the luminous dial of my watch, since the numbers seemed to stand out like electric lights.

We fully expected that the Japanese patrol, which killed Stevenson, would follow the boys who fled the camp as they made their way down the mountain. Because I only have one eye [Thorpe lost his right eye in a booby trap explosion in 1942], I was afraid that I might let the boys down by not seeing all that I should. Their lives were in my hands. However, I managed to convince myself that the bushes were not moving any closer by remembering something that I learned during training. And that was at night to always focus your vision above an object, but really see only what is underneath. If by any chance the enemy had come within 50 yards of the village, they would have heard a hell of a racket. The men were snoring so loudly that it was a wonder they did not wake each other up.

While all these thoughts were going through my mind, I was suddenly startled by a loud explosion inside the compound. The snoring stopped abruptly. The soldiers shot out from the hut where they were sleeping—their guns at the ready. I had visions of a Jap patrol scaling the cliff behind the village. But all I could see was a dense cloud of smoke and ashes emanating from under the hut where the natives were sleeping. An eerie quiet momentarily descended on the camp. Then a voice shouted out in Pidgin English, "Masta! Masta! Cartridge belong me—fire up!"

These natives only wear a loincloth, and they sleep curled up around their fires with their hands between their legs. When one half of the body gets warm, they turn over and do the other side. Kiabi was wearing a wide leather belt that had slits to carry his .303 ammunition. A cartridge had gone off in his belt and blew the back of his left hand off. We quickly patched the wound with sulfa powder and bandage.

There was no more sleep for anyone that night, so we loaded up the carriers we had and proceeded down the mountain. We soon came to the edge of a deep gorge. Across the ravine, at about 150 yards, was a Seventh-Day Adventist village. We observed the settlement for some time. Everything looked peaceful. The villagers were busy going about their everyday chores. Two natives were sweeping the ground with birch brooms. We decided to give it a go, and perhaps be able to buy some food.

Our party started down to the gorge. We estimated that it would take about an hour or so to get to the riverbed and two more hours to climb to the village. When we reached the bottom of the ravine, two police boys led the way up the steep slope. They were followed by our men, and then the carriers with the teleradio. I brought up the rear. We had only climbed for about 20 minutes when rifle shots rang out—then two sudden bursts of machine-gun fire. There was much shouting and confusion. The native carriers panicked and began slipping and sliding back down the bluff. They dropped all our gear, including the teleradio. I tried to stop one of the fleeing natives to find out what had happened, but he was coming too fast and swung at me with his machete. I let the other carriers go, and eventually the rest of our group gathered at the bottom of the gorge.

Apparently there was a large Japanese patrol in the village. Our forward scout shot two enemy soldiers, while others poured out from various huts in the settlement.

The last message received, before the radio was lost, was that we had three weeks to reach the west coast and be evacuated. There would be a lot of hostile country to negotiate, and some of the highest mountains in Bougainville. We decided to put as much distance between us and the Japs as possible. All rivers lead to the sea, so we headed downstream along the gorge—jumping from rock to rock. Some of the rock pools were deeper than I thought. I jumped into one that must have been ten feet deep. With all the gear I was carrying—eight magazines for my tommy gun, four grenades, my pack, and the gun itself—I sank like a stone. I was crawling along the bottom like a crab, when a police boy dived in, grabbed my hand, and hauled me to the surface. As soon as I climbed out of the water, I discarded my pack and anything else that was not essential.

The Japs, from the village above, were running along the top of the cliff. They began dropping mortar bombs around us, which detonated on contact with the rocks, but none of our men were hit. We soon outdistanced the enemy.

There were a lot of things that happened to us, and, when one thinks of them afterwards—even the urgent and serious situations—there was always a laugh to be had later on. We had some very close shaves—five ambushes in three days—with Lieutenant Stevenson killed and two men wounded. I was 21 years old at the time.

CHAPTER 14

Escape from Bougainville: The U.S.S. *Guardfish* Rescues

JULY 20–JULY 30, 1943

Jack Keenan and Jack Read

On July 20, 1943, Paul Mason was notified by Station KEN that the evacuation would take place on the night of the 24th at a specified point on Atsinima Bay. Besides Mason and Keenan, 60 other people were anxiously awaiting rescue. The evacuees comprised 22 soldiers, two airmen, eight Chinese, nine police boys, and 19 loyal natives.

The night before the submarine's arrival, a sentry was posted on each approach to the beach with orders to report any Japanese activity in the area. The next morning, a white calico sheet was tied to a couple of trees near the shoreline to point out the evacuation site for the rescue vessel. Lieutenant Keenan described the dramatic scene:

At dusk, everyone had assembled at the beach. The signal fire was lighted, and, at approximately 8 P.M., the silhouette of a submarine, the U.S.S. *Guardfish*, could easily be seen lying about 400 yards offshore. We did not have canoes and waited for word from the sub. About an hour later, a rubber boat was sighted heading toward shore. Other rafts followed close behind.

When the first boat reached the beach, the officer in charge reported that he had instructions to evacuate only 50 people. I explained our situation and decided to return with the officer to the submarine. I hoped to convince the captain to take the entire group of people waiting on the beach. I decided to take the teleradio with me to the ship, but the heavy surf capsized the boat and I lost the wireless. We scrambled back into the boat and paddled out to the *Guardfish.*

I asked the skipper, Lieutenant Commander Norvell G. Ward, if it was possible to increase the number of evacuees. He finally agreed to take 60 people. But before I was able to send word back to the beach, Mason arrived at the submarine in the rubber rafts containing 48 refugees—the original figure of 50 including ourselves. Unfortunately, 12 natives were left behind.

[Shortly before midnight, the *Guardfish* got underway and headed out to sea.] The officers and crew of the submarine made us as comfortable as possible. We dove just before dawn and then traveled submerged until about midday. After surfacing for ten minutes, we dove again and stayed submerged for the remainder of the day.

The *Guardfish* surfaced after dark and continued in a southerly direction. About 5 A.M., we rendezvoused with a sub-chaser that was to take us to Guadalcanal. By dawn, we had all been transferred aboard the small ship, and we watched the sub as it turned north toward Bougainville to evacuate Jack Read and his party.

As we headed south, I could see, in the early morning darkness, antiaircraft shells bursting over Munda. As dawn broke, the southern end of New Georgia Island came into view, and throughout the day we watched as swarms of Allied aircraft attacked enemy positions. It was a thrilling sight to see planes that were not Japanese. The natives, many of whom had never seen one of our aircraft, could not believe that all those planes were on our side.

It was about dusk when we passed Cape Esperance, Guadalcanal. I was sorry that we did not pass along the coast of the island at daylight, so that the natives could see with their own eyes the number of wrecked Japanese ships and planes that littered the shore.

On its second trip to Bougainville the Guardfish *evacuated 23 people. In addition to Jack Read, the rescued personnel included Captain Eric Robinson, Usaia Sotutu, Anton Jossten, Sergeant Yauwika, Corporal Sali, Constables Sanei and Ena, and 15 other natives. The site chosen for the rescue of Jack Read and his party was at a point south of the Kiviki River. At 4 A.M., on July 30, Read and his men were transferred to a subchaser, and at 7 P.M., they reached Guadalcanal.*
Read stated:

Usaia Sotutu and Anton Jossten arrived with extra natives to aid us in reaching the coast. My group was intact, with the exception of Bobby Pitt and the married people. They arrived at Kunua ahead of me and took it upon themselves to head farther south. They were not on hand when the *Guardfish* returned to pick us up on the night of July 28. Consequently, my party was considerably smaller than anticipated.

My first intimation of the ship's presence was the sudden appearance on the beach of a half-dozen inflated rafts. They were guided to shore by our prearranged signal fires. The embarkation was effected in a matter of minutes, and I was able to renew my acquaintance with Lieutenant Commander Ward. The last time we met was on the bridge of the *Gato* in the darkness of Teop Harbor.

CHAPTER 15

Epilogue

Jack Read and Paul Mason

Jack Read summarized his many months as a coast watcher with the following comments:

It had actually been a pretty hard existence on Bougainville—such as few realize. Still, I would have been more satisfied to see the job through until the Americans landed at Empress Augusta Bay in November. However, that was not possible.

Reviewing the course of our operations, coast watching on that most northerly peg of the Solomons had fulfilled its mission long before we were driven out—and to a far greater effect than even we realized. During the early and uncertain days of the American struggle to wrest Guadalcanal from the Japanese, the reports and timely warnings from Stations JEF and STO on Bougainville were directly responsible for the enemy's defeat.

Paul Mason concluded his report with the following statement:

Admiral William Halsey praised the work of the coast watchers, and said that the intelligence information forwarded from Bougainville by Lieutenant Read and myself had saved Guadalcanal—and that Guadalcanal had saved the South Pacific.

Afterword

Commander Eric Feldt, in his book, accurately described Paul: "41 years old, short, serious, and bespectacled. However, his appearance was deceptive. He was also tough, self-reliant, and calculating. Although a loner, Paul Mason was very much a man of decision and action."

Jack Read was five years younger, and more of an extrovert. At first, both men were a little wary of each other, but they soon became fast friends. They worked well together.

Paul spent more than half his life in Bougainville and other Solomon Islands, and he was skilled in handling the local people. He had studied the natives for a long period of time and knew their ways. During the war, one of his guerrilla fighters remarked that Paul was always the last to eat after sharing his food with his black comrades. He treated their wounds and illnesses, and he took particular care of the native women and children. Paul had a saying, "Courtesy is understood in any language."

On one occasion, when he was a youngster in the islands, Paul was looking after a plantation for a person who had left for Sydney on a holiday. A copra ship entered the harbor, and the captain of the vessel approached Paul and said, "Send for the manager, laddie." Paul answered with dignity, his voice having not yet broken, "I *am* the manager!"

Paul Mason got along extremely well with Otton and Wigley, and recommended them for decorations. However, there were certain members of both groups of soldiers who did not meet with his approval. It was a difficult task, leading those untried men through Japanese-held territory. He had to look after them as well as himself. Paul was a staunch believer in the old adage, "He travels fastest who travels alone." He was very much a man of his times and mores.

Another interesting story about Paul Mason concerns his relationship with Toshiro, who was in Japanese intelligence during the war and may have saved Paul's life. After Wong You was captured by the enemy, the Chinese merchant was interrogated by a Japanese officer who inquired as to Paul's whereabouts. Toshiro intervened and said, "How can you expect this man, who has known Mason for 20 years, to betray him to you—a person he has only known for 20 minutes." Paul often wondered about Toshiro. Could he have put the Japanese on the trail of the coast watchers at other times—but did not?

Paul's reports were very pragmatic. He just put down the facts. Jack Read, however, was captivated by the beauty of the Sohano area. It was not that Paul was indifferent. He knew that Bougainville was the most beautiful place in the world. He had known this for many years, while Jack, on the other hand, had just arrived on the island.

One of the saddest stories of the early coast watching days was the execution of Boros by the Japanese. Boros was the *tul-tul* of a village near Kieta. He had said to Paul, "I will never betray you or any of the coast watchers, even if they cut off my head." And they did.

Paul had a little stone set for Boros in front of the larger Australian memorial at Kieta. It just says, "In memory of Boros, a loyal native."

I felt the loyalty of the people of Bougainville toward Paul very touching. Of course, near the end, with the Japanese Army hounding them, it was very hard for the natives to remain loyal. Especially when they saw the coast watchers on the run—hiding and being hunted up and down the island by the Japanese.

The fact that Paul and Jack managed to keep the loyalty of those few who stuck by them to the end is a great tribute to them both—and to the natives and police boys who shared the hardships and dangers.

Noelle Mason

Military and Police Personnel on Buka and Bougainville

AUSTRALIAN IMPERIAL FORCE (AIF—ARMY) PERSONNEL

Lieutenant Mackie's Detachment

Lieutenant J. Mackie
Sergeant A. Leyden
Corporal H. Cameron
Corporal W. Dolby
Corporal A. Jamieson
Corporal D. McLean
Corporal J. Wigley
Lance Corporal J. Matthews
Lance Corporal K. Warner
Sapper Douglas Otton
Signalman H. Brown
Signalman D. L. Sly
Private D. Ellam

Private C. Francis
Private L. Johnston
Private J. McDonnell
Private J. McGarrell
Private A. McNab
Private N. Randall
Private W. Ross
Private B. Swanson
Private Neil Thompson
Private H. Tulloch
Private M. Waterhouse
Private B. White
Private V. Wills

Lieutenant Bedkober's Detachment

Lieutenant D. Bedkober
S/Sergeant B. Cohen
Sergeant H. Broadfoot
Sergeant J. Collier
Sergeant W. Florance
L/Sergeant N. Martin
A/Sergeant V. Day
A/Sergeant F. Furner

A/Corporal N. McLeod
Sapper D. Ayliffe
Sapper B. Bostick
Sapper R. Cassidy
Sapper S. Gage
Sapper C. McKenzie
Signalman R. Cream
Signalman A. Eastlake

A/Sergeant A. Hatherly
A/Sergeant G. McPhee
A/Sergeant Walter Radimey
A/Sergeant Ken Thorpe
A/Corporal A. Little

Signalman A. Falls
Signalman G. Kotz
Signalman E. Rust
Private S. Stonehouse
Private H. Woods

ROYAL AUSTRALIAN AIR FORCE PERSONNEL: THE CATALINA FLIGHT CREW

Flight Lieutenant W. J. Clark
Flight Officer C. S. Dunn
Flight Officer J. N. Potts
Sergeant F. G. Thompson
Sergeant D. J. Ward
Pilot Officer C. J. Twist
Corporal J. Fenwick
Corporal H. Yates
Corporal R. N. Wettenhall

BOUGAINVILLE AND BUKA NATIVE CONSTABULARY (POLICE BOYS)

Sergeant Kanusi
Sergeant Waramabi
Sergeant Yauwika
Corporal Abui
Constable Ena
Constable Iamulu
Constable Kiabi
Constable Kiniwai
Constable Lunga
Constable Maia
Constable Matu

Corporal Auna
Corporal Sali
Corporal Sanei
Corporal Buia
Constable Meikuk
Constable Meimbunga
Constable Moitaka
Constable Namora
Constable Owanda
Constable Rankis

Index

Page numbers in italics indicate illustrations.

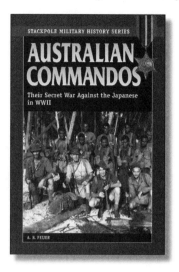

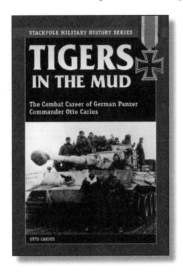

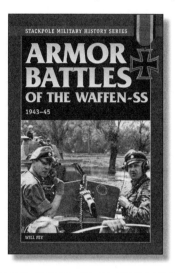